e✓eryday

Vocabulary
Intervention Activities

Table of Contents

Using Everyday Vocabulary Intervention Activities

Current research identifies vocabulary and word study as essential skills for reading success. Before children learn to read, they need to be aware of the meaning of words. Vocabulary instruction teaches children how to determine the meanings of words by utilizing contextual and conceptual clues. Word-study and word-solving strategies help children build their vocabularies, which leads to increased reading comprehension.

Effective vocabulary activities provide students with opportunities to:

- Actively engage in learning more about words and how words work

- Build their vocabularies and gain greater control of language

- Develop the ability to use context clues to define unfamiliar words

- Develop and build content vocabulary

Although some students master these skills easily during regular classroom instruction, many others need additional re-teaching opportunities to master these essential skills. The Everyday Vocabulary Intervention Activities series provides easy-to-use, five-day intervention units for Grades K–5. These units are structured around a research-based Model-Guide-Practice-Apply approach. You can use these activities in a variety of intervention models, including Response to Intervention (RTI).

Everyday Vocabulary Intervention Activities Grade 2 • ©2011 Newmark Learning, LLC

Getting Started

In just five simple steps, *Everyday Vocabulary Intervention Activities* provides everything you need to identify students' needs and to provide targeted intervention.

online

1. PRE-ASSESS to identify students' vocabulary needs.

Use the pre-assessment to identify the skills your students need to master.

Day 1

2. MODEL the skill.

Every five-day unit targets a specific vocabulary and word study. On Day 1, use the teacher prompts and reproducible activity page to introduce and model the skill.

Day 2   **Day 3**   **Day 4**

3. GUIDE, PRACTICE, and APPLY.

Use the reproducible practice activities for Days 2, 3, and 4 to build students' understanding and skill-proficiency.

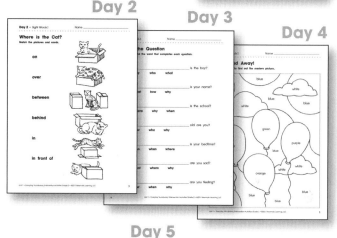

Day 5

4. MONITOR progress.

Administer the Day 5 reproducible assessment to monitor each student's progress and to make instructional decisions.

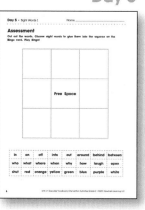

5. POST-ASSESS to document student progress.

Use the post-assessment to measure students' progress as a result of your interventions.

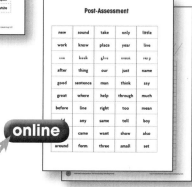

online

Standards-Based Vocabulary Awareness Skills in Everyday Intervention Activities

The vocabulary words and strategies found in the Everyday Intervention Activities series are introduced developmentally and spiral from one grade to the next. The chart below shows the types of words and skill areas addressed at each grade level in this series.

Everyday Vocabulary Intervention Activities Series Skills	K	1	2	3	4	5
Sight Words	✔	✔	✔	✔		
Nouns, Pronouns, and Proper Nouns	✔	✔	✔	✔	✔	✔
Verbs	✔	✔	✔	✔	✔	✔
Adjectives	✔	✔	✔	✔	✔	✔
Synonyms and Antonyms	✔	✔	✔	✔	✔	✔
Compound Words		✔	✔	✔	✔	✔
Multiple-Meaning Words	✔	✔	✔	✔	✔	✔
Classify Words by Subject	✔	✔	✔	✔	✔	✔
Word Analogies	✔	✔	✔	✔	✔	✔
Word Parts and Root Words	✔	✔	✔	✔	✔	✔
Word Webs and Diagrams	✔	✔	✔	✔	✔	✔
Using Words in Context	✔	✔	✔	✔	✔	✔
Using Context Clues to Determine Word Meaning				✔	✔	✔
Language Arts Content Words	✔	✔	✔	✔	✔	✔
Social Studies Content Words	✔	✔	✔	✔	✔	✔
Science Content Words	✔	✔	✔	✔	✔	✔
Math Content Words	✔	✔	✔	✔	✔	✔

Everyday Vocabulary Intervention Activities Grade 2 • ©2011 Newmark Learning, LLC

Using Everyday Intervention for RTI

According to the National Center on Response to Intervention, RTI "integrates assessment and intervention within a multi-level prevention system to maximize student achievement and to reduce behavior problems." This model of instruction and assessment allows schools to identify at-risk students, monitor their progress, provide research-proven interventions, and "adjust the intensity and nature of those interventions depending on a student's responsiveness."

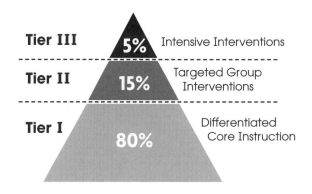

RTI models vary from district to district, but the most prevalent model is a three-tiered approach to instruction and assessment.

The Three Tiers of RTI	Using Everyday Intervention Activities
Tier I: Differentiated Core Instruction • Designed for all students • Preventive, proactive, standards-aligned instruction • Whole- and small-group differentiated instruction • Ninety-minute, daily core reading instruction in the five essential skill areas: phonics, phonemic awareness, comprehension, vocabulary, fluency	• Use whole-group vocabulary mini-lessons to introduce and guide practice with vocabulary strategies that all students need to learn. • Use any or all of the units in the order that supports your core instructional program.
Tier II: Targeted Group Interventions • For at-risk students • Provide thirty minutes of daily instruction beyond the ninety-minute Tier I core reading instruction • Instruction is conducted in small groups of three to five students with similar needs	• Select units based on your students' areas of need (the pre-assessment can help you identify these). • Use the units as week-long, small-group mini-lessons.
Tier III: Intensive Interventions • For high-risk students experiencing considerable difficulty in reading • Provide up to sixty minutes of additional intensive intervention each day in addition to the ninety-minute Tier I core reading instruction • More intense and explicit instruction • Instruction conducted individually or with smaller groups of one to three students with similar needs	• Select units based on your students' areas of need. • Use the units as one component of an intensive vocabulary intervention program.

Everyday Vocabulary Intervention Activities Grade 2 • ©2011 Newmark Learning, LLC

Overview Sight Words I

Directions and Sample Answers for Activity Pages

Day 1	See "Provide a Real-World Example" below.
Day 2	Read aloud the title and directions. Help students read each word in the left-hand column. Then guide them to find the matching picture in the right-hand column, and draw a line between the two.
Day 3	Read aloud the title and directions. Review the question words: **who**, **what**, **where**, **when**, **why**, and **how**. Help students read the questions using the different possible answers. Guide them to identify and draw a circle around the correct word for each question.
Day 4	Read aloud the title and directions. Provide crayons. Help students read the names of the colors. Then encourage them to color in the spaces to reveal the mystery picture (balloons in the sky).
Day 5	Prepare by writing the words on scraps of paper and putting them in a container. Tell students to select eight of the twenty-four words to cut out and glue onto their Bingo cards. Explain that you will pick a word from the container, write it on the board, and read it aloud. If a word you read matches a word on the card they are using, they should draw an X on the box. Tell them to say "Bingo" when they get three in a row.

Provide a Real-World Example

◆ Close the classroom door. **Say:** *The door is shut*. Write the word **shut** on chart paper. Now open the door. **Say:** *Now the door is open*. Write **open** on chart paper.

◆ Walk out the door and then walk back in. **Ask:** *What did I just do?* Write **what** on the chart paper or the board. (Allow responses.) Then **say:** *Yes, I walked through the door.* Write **through** on the chart paper. *Where did I go?* Write **where** on the chart paper. (Allow responses.) **Say:** *I walked into the hallway.* Write **into** on the chart paper. Then **say:** *I walked back into the classroom again.* Write **again** on the chart paper. Then say each word aloud again. **Say:** *We use these words all of the time. We use these when we talk, write, and read.*

◆ Hand out the Day 1 activity page. **Say:** *Let's look at more words we see and say all the time.* Draw students' attention to the girl crossing the monkey bars. **Say:** *She is going across.* Repeat the word **across**. *Let's trace and write the word **across**.*

◆ Draw attention to the merry-go-round. **Say:** *The children are going around and around. Let's trace and write the word **around**.* After students trace and write the word, **say:** *Look at the children laugh. Let's trace and write the word **laugh**.*

◆ Repeat with other examples.

Sight Words

shut   again

open   across

what   around

through   laugh

where

into

All Around the Playground

Trace each word. Write the word on the line.

Name _____

Where is the Cat?

Match the pictures and words.

on

over

between

behind

in

in front of

Complete the Question

Draw a circle around the word that completes each question.

_____ is the boy?

Why   **Who**   **What**

_____ is your name?

What   **How**   **Why**

_____ is the school?

Where   **Why**   **When**

_____ old are you?

How   **Who**   **Why**

_____ is your bedtime?

Who   **When**   **Where**

_____ are you sad?

What   **Where**   **Why**

_____ are you feeling?

How   **When**   **Why**

Up, Up, and Away!

Color each space to find out the mystery picture.

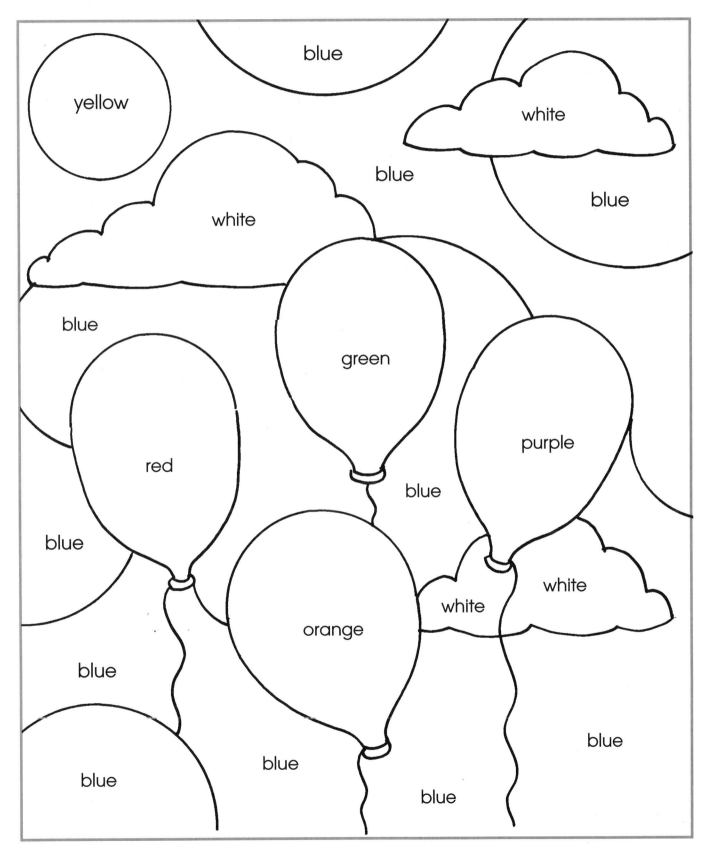

Assessment

Cut out the words. Choose eight words to glue into the squares on the Bingo card. Play Bingo!

	Free Space	

in	on	off	into	out	around
behind	between	who	what	where	when
why	how	laugh	open	shut	red
orange	yellow	green	blue	purple	white

Unit 1 • Everyday Vocabulary Intervention Activities Grade 2 • ©2011 Newmark Learning, LLC

Overview   Nouns, Pronouns, and Possessives

Directions and Sample Answers for Activity Pages

Day 1	See "Provide a Real-World Example" below.
Day 2	Read aloud the title and directions. Help students cut out the pictures. Guide them to identify each as **she**, **he**, or **they**. Then help them glue the pictures in the right column. (**She:** mom, sister, grandmother; **He:** dad, brother, grandfather; **They:** family; mom and dad; sisters)
Day 3	Read aloud the title and directions. Help students find a trail made entirely of things. Guide them to identify each picture as a person, place, or thing. Help them draw a line to show the trail of things that will lead the kids to their home.
Day 4	Read aloud the title and directions. Review with students that a proper noun names a specific person, place, or thing. Give a few examples such as days of the week, months, names, etc. Then have them complete each sentence by writing a proper noun. Help with spelling as needed.
Day 5	Read aloud the title and directions. Allow time for students to complete the task. Afterward, meet individually with students to discuss their results. Use their responses to plan further instruction and review.

Provide a Real-World Example

◆ **Say:** *I am Mr. / Ms. / Mrs. (insert your name). I am your teacher.* Write **I**, **your**, and **teacher** on chart paper or the board. Now hold up a pencil and **say:** *This is my pencil. It is sharp.* Write **my**, **pencil**, and **it** on the chart paper. Now **say:** *This is our school. We like our school.* Write **our**, **school**, and **we** on the chart paper, too.

◆ Point to the words **teacher**, **pencil**, and **school** and **say:** *These words name a person (teacher), a place (school), and a thing (pencil). Naming words are called nouns.* Point to the words **I**, **it**, and **we**. **Say:** *We use these words in place of nouns.* Now point to the words **your**, **my**, and **our**. **Say:** *These words name who has or owns something.*

◆ Hand out the Day 1 activity page. Direct students' attention to the first picture. **Say:** *A flag is a thing. Let's draw a line to the word **thing**.* Now trace the word **flag**. Next, look at the girl. **Say:** *She is a person. Let's draw a line to the word **person**.* Now trace the word **she**. Finally, direct attention to the sign for the zoo. **Ask:** *Is a zoo a person, place, or thing?* (Allow responses.) **Say:** *Yes, a zoo is a place. Let's draw a line to "place" and trace the word **zoo**.* Now instruct students to draw one person, one place, and one thing and label each.

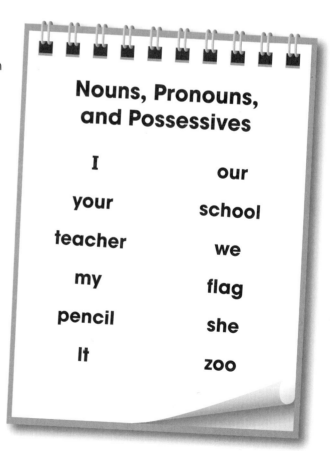

Nouns, Pronouns, and Possessives

I	our
your	school
teacher	we
my	flag
pencil	she
It	zoo

Person, Place, or Thing

Draw a line from each picture to the correct box (person, place or thing).

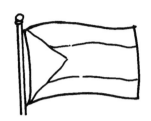

_____

_____

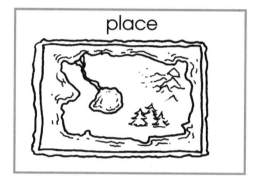

Draw a person, place, and thing in each box. Label your pictures.

person	place	thing

She, He, or They?

Cut out the pictures. Glue the pictures under She, He, or They.

She	He	They

Lost in the Woods

The kids made a trail of things to find their way home. They are lost! Find the path made up of things and help them find their way home.

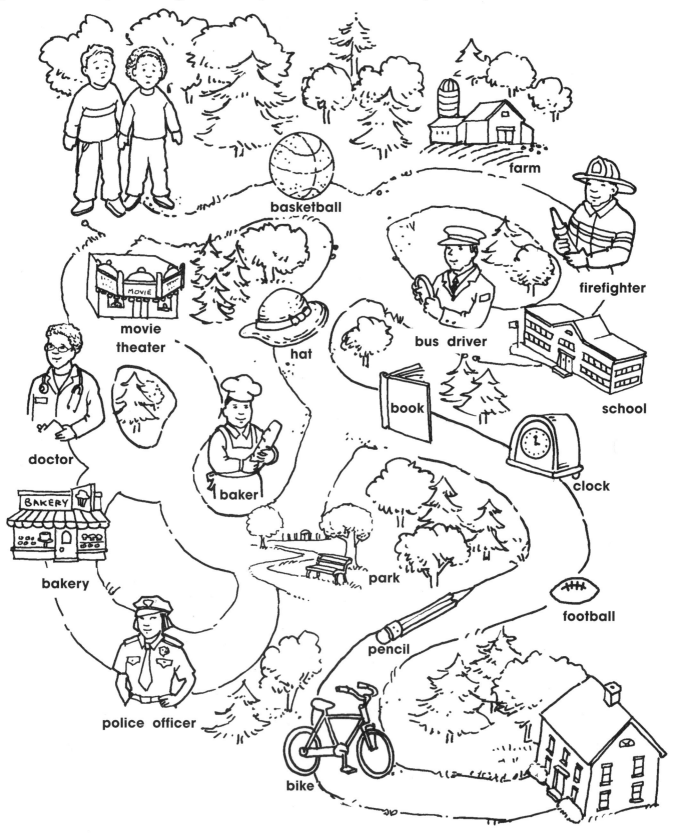

School Days

Write a proper noun to complete each sentence.

Our teacher is _____.

Our principal is _____.

We have art class on _____.

We have music class on _____.

The name of our school is _____.

School begins in _____.

We do not come to school on _____.

Assessment

Draw a line to match pictures and words.

their hats

my hat

his hat

its hat

her hat

   Unit 2 • Everyday Vocabulary Intervention Activities Grade 2 • ©2011 Newmark Learning, LLC

Overview   Action Words/Verbs

Directions and Sample Answers for Activity Pages

Day 1	See "Provide a Real-World Example" below.
Day 2	Read aloud the title and directions. Read aloud each sentence and the two possible answers. Guide students to use the context clues to figure out which verb is correct. Then help them draw a circle around the correct verb.
Day 3	Read aloud the title and directions. Review the meaning of present and past tense verbs and give an example such as **I stand today. I stood yesterday.** Help them cut out the verbs at the bottom, and guide them to identify which word completes each sentence. Help them glue the words in the boxes.
Day 4	Read aloud the title and directions. Help students identify the picture clues. Show them how to use the words in the word list to confirm their answers. Model how to write the words into the crossword puzzle.
Day 5	Read aloud the title and directions. Allow time for students to complete the task. Afterward, meet individually with students to discuss their results. Use their responses to plan further instruction and review.

Provide a Real-World Example

◆ Run into the classroom. **Ask:** *What am I doing?* (Allow responses.) Write **run** on chart paper or the board and **say:** *Run is an action word. An action word is called a verb. A verb tells what someone is doing.*

◆ **Ask:** *How does a bird get from one place to another?* (Allow responses.) Write **fly** on the list and **say:** *Fly is a verb.*

◆ **Say:** *I hope you understand what a verb is.* Write **hope** on the chart paper and **say:** *Hope is a verb. Verbs can tell what a person is thinking, too.* Invite students to think of action words/verbs. Add their words to the list.

◆ Hand out the Day 1 activity page and crayons. **Say:** *This castle is full of verbs. The witch flies on her broom. Fly is a verb. Color in the witch. Trace and write the word fly at the bottom. The princess looks at the frog. Look is a verb, too. Color in the princess. Trace and write the word look. The frog sits in the fruit bowl. Sit is a verb. Color in the frog and the fruit. Trace and write the word sit. The person blows a horn. Blow is a verb. Color in the person blowing the horn. Trace and write the word blow.*

Action Words

run

fly

hope

look

sit

blow

Name _____

Action at the Castle

Look at the picture. Listen to your teacher. Color the pictures. Trace and write the words.

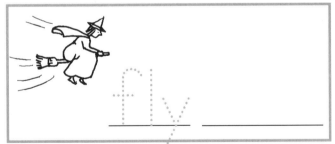

fly
___ ___

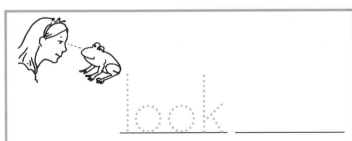

look
___ ___

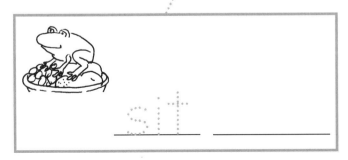

sit
___ ___

blow
___ ___

Finish the Sentence

Read each sentence. Draw a circle around the verb that best completes the sentence.

I _____ a

book

read   eat

I _____ in a

bed

fly   sleep

I _____ to

school

laugh   walk

I _____ on the

telephone

talk   walk

I _____ a

cup

sleep   hold

I _____ fast!

run   shout

Past and Present

Cut out the verbs. Glue the verbs in the boxes to make sentences.
Use the clues to help you know if the word is in the present or past.

		Clues
I [ ] a joke today.		to tell
I [ ] in a chair today.		to sit
I [ ] a coin today.		to find
I [ ] a letter today.		to write
I [ ] joke yesterday.		to tell
I [ ] in a chair yesterday.		to sit
I [ ] a coin yesterday.		to find
I [ ] a letter yesterday.		to write

find	found	sat	sit
tell	told	write	wrote

Verb Crossword

Look at the pictures. Find the verb in the word list. Fill in the crossword puzzle.

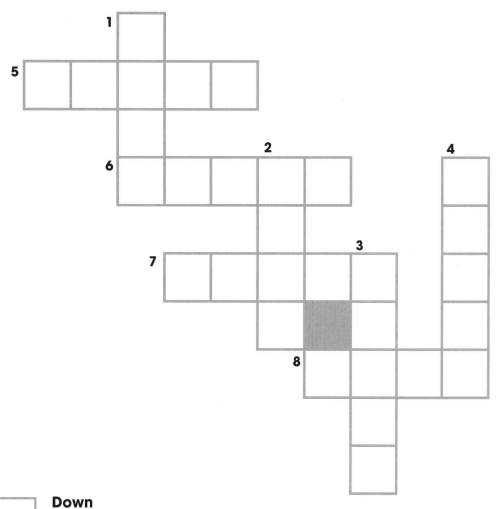

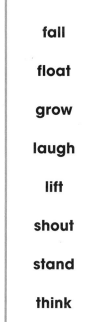

fall
float
grow
laugh
lift
shout
stand
think

Down

Across

Assessment

Draw a line to match the verbs to the pictures.

sleep

laugh

write

read

sit

think

run

fly

lift

look

Overview Adjectives and Adverbs

Directions and Sample Answers for Activity Pages

Day 1	See "Provide a Real-World Example" below.
Day 2	Read aloud the title and directions. Explain that we use adjectives to describe feelings. Help students to identify what feeling each face expresses. Then help them find that word and draw a line between the face and the word.
Day 3	Read aloud the title and directions. Remind students that colors are adjectives because they describe what something looks like. Help students read and color in each flower.
Day 4	Read aloud the title and directions. Explain that we use adjectives to describe how things taste. Discuss foods students know that are salty, sweet, bitter, and sour. Read the name of each food on the chart. Have students identify what that food tastes like by checking a column. Then guide students to draw their favorite food and label it as salty, sweet, bitter, or sour.
Day 5	Read aloud the directions. Allow time for students to complete the task. Afterward, meet individually with students to discuss their results. Use their responses to plan further instruction and review.

Provide a Real-World Example

◆ Point to the wall clock and **say:** *The clock is round.* Write **round** on the chart paper or the board. Touch the glass of a classroom window and **say:** *The window is smooth and cool.* Write **smooth** and **cool** on the chart paper.

◆ **Say: *Round**, **smooth**, and **cool** are words we use to describe nouns—the clock and the window. Words that describe, or tell about nouns, are called adjectives. Adjectives describe shape, size, color, feelings, the weather, and more. Look around the classroom. What other adjectives can you think of?* List students' ideas on the chart paper.

◆ Now walk very slowly around the room. **Say:** *I am walking slowly.* Now walk quickly around the room and **say:** *Now I am walking quickly. **Slowly** and **quickly** are words we use to describe actions or verbs. We call these words **adverbs**.*

◆ Hand out the Day 1 activity page. Read aloud the directions. Help students with the first few examples. Read the words ***sunny day*** and **ask:** *What does **sunny** describe?* (Allow responses.) *Yes, sunny describes the day. Let's circle the word **sunny**. Let's write **sunny** on the line.*

Adjectives and Adverbs

round

smooth

cool

slowly

quickly

sunny

Find It, Circle It

Look at the words. Look at the picture. Circle the describing word in each phrase.
Write the word on the line.

sunny day

_____

hot tea

_____

run quickly

_____

tall boy

_____

sleepy baby

_____

jump suddenly

_____

high kite

_____

Match-an-Emotion

Draw a line from each face to the word that best describes it.

worried

sleepy

happy

angry

sad

Color-a-Garden

Read the word on each flower, and color it in that color.

          Unit 4 • Everyday Vocabulary Intervention Activities Grade 2 • ©2011 Newmark Learning, LLC

Name _____

Flavor Checklist

Look at the food items. Decide if each food is salty, sweet, bitter, or sour.
Check the box.

	Salty	Sweet	Bitter	Sour
lemon				
ice cream				
pretzel				
coffee				
popcorn				
pickle				
watermelon				

Draw your favorite food. Label it as salty, sweet, bitter, or sour.

Assessment

Draw a line between each describing word and its opposite.

angry	cool
high	dry
wet	light
tall	low
dark	slowly
warm	happy
quickly	short

Overview Contractions and Compound Words

Directions and Sample Answers for Activity Pages

Day 1	See "Provide a Real-World Example" below.
Day 2	Read aloud the title and directions. Help students read the sentences and identify the missing word from the two choices. Guide them to draw a circle around the correct word and write it on the line.
Day 3	Read aloud the title and directions. Read aloud the words in each column with students. Guide them to find words from each column that when put together make a compound word. Guide them to draw a line between the words.
Day 4	Read aloud the title and directions. Help students identify the picture clues. Show them how to use the words in the word list to confirm their answers. Model how to write the word into the crossword puzzle.
Day 5	Read aloud the title and directions. Allow time for students to complete the task. Afterward, meet individually with students to discuss their results. Use their responses to plan further instruction and review.

Provide a Real-World Example

◆ **Say:** *I don't like peanut butter.* Write the word **don't** on chart paper or the board. **Say: Don't** *is really two words:* **do** *and* **not**. On the board, write the words **do** and **not**. Explain that to make the word **don't**, you replace the **o** in **not** with an apostrophe. Write the word **don't** again to model how to do this and what an apostrophe is. Explain that we call this kind of word a contraction. Now **say:** *I'll eat a carrot.* Write **I'll** on the chart paper. **Say: I'll** *is a contraction, too. It is made up of two words,* **I** *and* **will**. *In this word, the apostrophe replaces the letters* **w** *and* **i** *in* **will**. Model on the board how **I will** becomes **I'll**.

◆ **Say:** *Everyone in our classroom loves carrots!* Write **everyone** and **classroom** on the chart paper. **Say: Everyone** *and* **classroom** *are also each made up of two words.* **Everyone** *includes the words* **every** *and* **one**. *But there is no apostrophe in* **everyone**, *and we don't remove any letters. Words made up of two complete words are called compound words. What words make up the compound word* **classroom**? (Allow responses.) **Say: Classroom** *is made up of the words* **class** *and* **room**.

◆ Hand out the Day 1 activity page. Model the first example. **Say: Did** *and* **not** *make the word* **didn't**. *We replace the* **o** *in* **not** *with an apostrophe. Let's write* **didn't**. Have students make a contraction with the words **have** and **not** and say aloud a sentence using the word.

◆ **Say:** *To make* **you** *and* **will** *a contraction, let's replace the* **wi** *with an apostrophe.* Write **you'll** on the line. **Say: They** *and* **have** *becomes* **they've** *by replacing* **h** *and* **a** *in* **have** *with an apostrophe.*

Contractions

don't   haven't

I'll   you'll

didn't   they've

Compounds

everyone

classroom

Contraction Add-traction!

Put the two words together to make a contraction. Then say a sentence using each new word.

1. did + not = _____

2. have + not = _____

3. you + will = _____

4. she + will = _____

5. they + have = _____

6. I + am = _____

7. it + is = _____

8. he + is = _____

9. we + are = _____

10. you + are = _____

Which Word Is It?

Listen to your teacher read the sentence. Draw a circle around the contraction that completes each sentence. Write the word on the line.

1. I _____ eat another bite!

    can't   **don't**

2. If Amy sleeps late, _____ miss the bus.

    she'll   **she's**

3. _____ in second grade.

    I'll   **I'm**

4. We _____ talk in the library.

    shouldn't   **should've**

5. I _____ won first prize if I ran faster.

    could've   **can't**

6. _____ cross the street without looking both ways.

    Can't   **Don't**

7. _____ the tallest boy in our class.

    We're   **He's**

8. _____ visiting our grandmother.

    We're   **We'll**

9. _____ going to the movies together.

    They've   **They're**

10. _____ a good dancer.

    She'll   **She's**

Make-a-Match

Draw a line between the two words to make a compound word. Then write the words next to the pictures at the bottom.

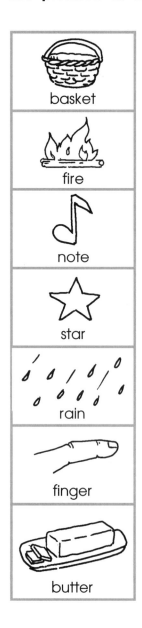

basket

fire

note

star

rain

finger

butter

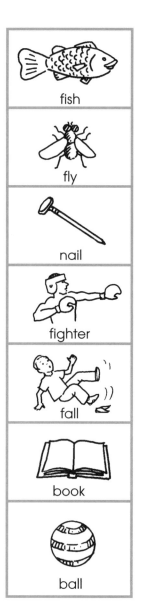

fish

fly

nail

fighter

fall

book

ball

_____

_____

_____

_____

_____

_____

_____

Compound Word Crossword Puzzle

Look at the pictures. Find the compound word in the word list. Fill in the crossword puzzle.

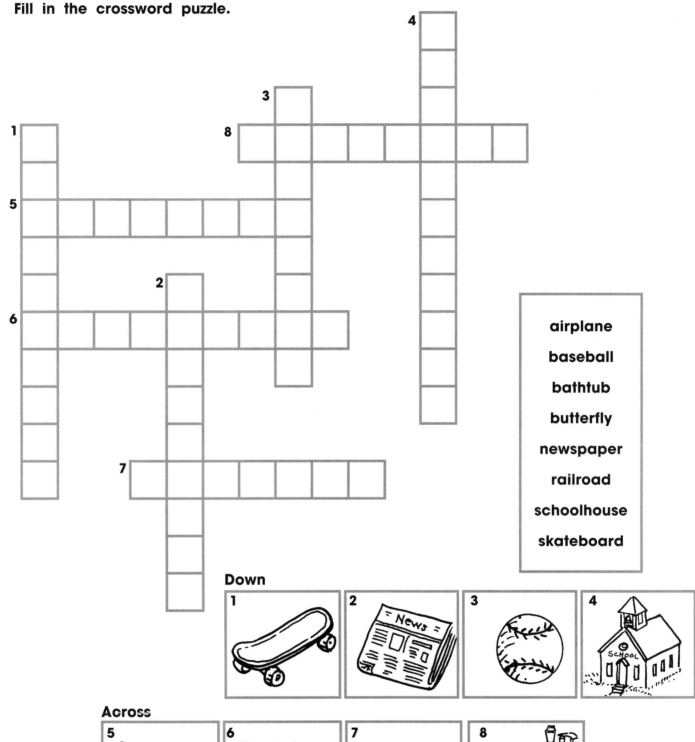

Word List

airplane

baseball

bathtub

butterfly

newspaper

railroad

schoolhouse

skateboard

Down

1. 2. 3. 4.

Across

5. 6. 7. 8.

Assessment

Choose a word from the word list to complete each sentence. Write it on the line.

_____ find his boots.

I _____ cry!

_____ given it a try.

_____ a tall woman.

He'll	I've	She's	won't

Put the words together to make a compound word. Then draw a picture to show each compound word's meaning.

butter + fly = _____

bath + tub = _____

school + house = _____

Overview Synonyms and Antonyms

Directions and Sample Answers for Activity Pages

Day 1	See "Provide a Real-World Example" below.
Day 2	Read aloud the title and directions. Help students cut out the scoops. Read the words on the scoops and the cones with students. Help them glue scoops onto cones with words that are synonyms.
Day 3	Read aloud the title and directions. Help students read the sentences, and find antonyms in the word list that complete each sentence. Guide them to write the word on the line.
Day 4	Read aloud the title and directions. Help students read each word. Then guide them to draw a line between each describing word and its opposite.
Day 5	Read aloud the title and directions. Allow time for students to complete the task. Afterward, meet individually with students to discuss their results. Use their responses to plan further instruction and review.

Provide a Real-World Example

◆ Invite a volunteer to the front of class. Hand the student a book and **say:** *I give you the book.* Write **give** on chart paper or the board. Then take the book back from the student. **Say:** *Now I take the book back from you.* Write **take** on chart paper. Explain that **give** and **take** have opposite meanings. **Say:** *We call words that have opposite meanings, like **give** and **take**, antonyms.*

◆ Shut the classroom door. **Ask:** *What did I just do?* (Allow responses.) Then **say:** *Yes, I closed the door. Another word that means the same as close is **shut**. Words that have the same meaning, like **close** and **shut**, are called synonyms.*

◆ Hand out the Day 1 activity page. Read aloud the directions. Model how to do the first one. Read aloud the two words: **young** and **old**. **Ask:** *Do **young** and **old** mean the same thing or do they have opposite meanings?* (Allow responses.) **Say:** *Young and old have opposite meanings. They are antonyms, so let's check the "Antonyms" column.*

Check It!

Read the word pairs. Check "Synonyms" if the words have the same meaning. Check "Antonyms" if they have opposite meanings.

	Antonyms	**Synonyms**
young/old	❑	❑
fast/quick	❑	❑
hard/soft	❑	❑
rough/bumpy	❑	❑
wet/dry	❑	❑
easy/simple	❑	❑
cold/cool	❑	❑
on/off	❑	❑

Name _____

Synonym Scoops

Cut out the ice cream scoops. Glue scoops on cones with words that have the same meaning.

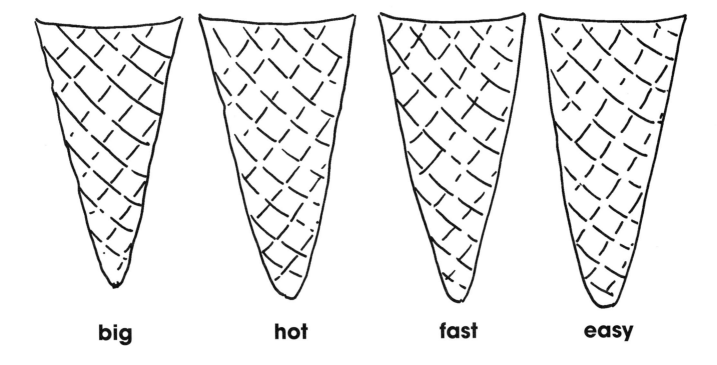

| big | hot | fast | easy |

| quick | large | simple | warm |

Find the Antonym

Choose a word from the word list to finish each sentence.
Write the word on the line.

fake	frown	hot	large	slow	soft	sour	young

1. She is not old. She is _____.

2. The car is fast. The turtle is _____.

3. The mouse is small. The elephant is _____.

4. The table is hard. The pillow is _____.

5. Sugar is sweet. Lemons are _____.

6. Winter is cold. Summer is _____.

7. When I'm happy I smile. When I'm sad I _____.

8. Is the coin real or _____?

Crazy Clue Matching

Draw a line between each describing word and its opposite.

old	smooth
cool	bent
dry	easy
off	wet
take	new
straight	give
bumpy	on
hard	warm

Assessment

Read each word. Then underline its synonym. Draw a circle around its antonym.

hot	cold	warm

large	big	small

fast	quick	slow

easy	hard	simple

rough	smooth	bumpy

shut	close	open

Overview Homonyms, Homographs, and Homophones

Directions and Sample Answers for Activity Pages

Day 1	See "Provide a Real-World Example" below.
Day 2	Read aloud the title and directions. Read aloud each sentence in the left-hand column with students. Help students find the picture in the right-hand column that matches the sentence.
Day 3	Read aloud the title and directions. Help students read the sentences. Then guide them to draw a circle around the homonym that correctly completes the sentence, and write the word on the line. (**Answers:** days, sea, rays, won, two, buy, high, ate)
Day 4	Read aloud the title and directions. Help students identify the clues. Then guide them to find the homonym for each clue in the word list. Help them write the word into the puzzle.
Day 5	Read aloud the title and directions. Allow time for students to complete the task. Afterward, meet individually with students to discuss their results. Use their responses to plan further instruction and review.

Provide a Real-World Example

◆ **Ask:** *Who came to school by car today?* Write the word **to** on the chart paper or the board. (Allow responses.) Then **say:** *I came to school by car today, too!* Write **too** on the chart paper. **Say:** *To and too sound the same, but they look different and they have different meanings.* **Ask:** *Does anyone know of another word that sounds the same as* **to** *and* **too**, *but has a different meaning?* (Allow responses.) *That's right!* **Two** *is also a number.* Write **two** on the chart paper. **Say:** *To, too, and two are called homonyms—words that sound the same, but have different spellings and different meanings.*

◆ Point to your watch and **say:** *This is a watch.* Now look at the class. **Say:** *I watch you.* Write **watch** on the chart paper. **Say:** *We spell both kinds of watch the same way. Watch is a homograph, or a word that is spelled the same way but has different meanings.*

◆ Hand out the Day 1 activity page. Direct students' attention to the first picture. **Say:** *This is a bear. We spell it b-e-a-r. The other word bare, spelled b-a-r-e, means not wearing clothes. Let's circle the first bear.* Repeat these steps for each picture, or if students are ready, they may work independently.

Homonyms, Homographs, and Homophones

to/too/two

watch

bear/bare

Picturing Homonyms

Circle the word that matches the picture.

1. bear   bare

2. won   one

3. meet   meat

4. nose   knows

5. rein   rain

6. sew   sow

7. four   for

8. pair   pear

Homograph Match-Up

Draw a line from each sentence to a picture.

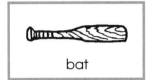
bat

She wore a bow in her hair.

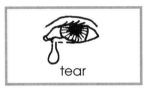
tear

A dove is a sign of peace.

bow

The swimmer dove into the pool.

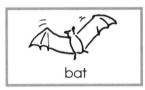
bat

Tear up the paper!

dove

The actor takes a bow.

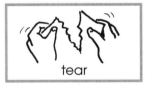
tear

I swung the bat.

dove

A tear ran down her cheek.

bow

A bat flew through the night sky.

Complete-a-Sentence

Read each sentence. Draw a circle around the correct homonym. Write it on the line.

1. There are _____ in a week.
   seven   **daze   days**

2. We  in the _____ .
   swim   **see   sea**

3. The sun's _____ are hot!
   rays   raise

4. Abby _____ the race!
   one   won

5. Jacob has _____  .
   two   too   dogs

6. We _____ clothes at the  .
   buy   by   store

7. The is _____ in the  .
   kite   **high   hi**   sky

8. Evan _____ a  .
   eight   ate   sandwich

Homonym Crossword

Look at each picture clue. Find the word in the word list. Write it into the puzzle.

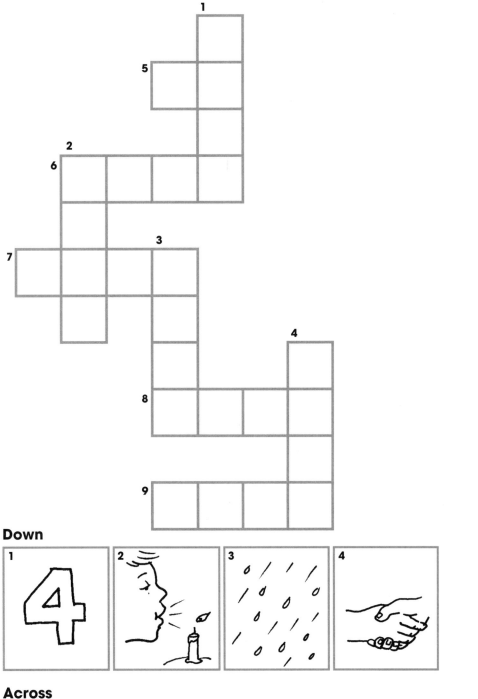

Word List
bear
blew
four
meet
no
nose
pear
rain
root

Down

Across

Assessment

Draw a circle around the homonym that completes the sentence.

1. I smell with my | **nose** | | **knows** | .

2. I | **sea** | | **see** | you!

3. I | **hear** | | **here** | with my ears.

4. Do you | **know** | | **no** | her?

Listen to your teacher. Draw a picture of what your teacher says. Label the picture with the homonym.

1	2	3

Overview   Language Arts Content Words

• •

Directions and Sample Answers for Activity Pages

Day 1	See "Provide a Real-World Example" below.
Day 2	Read aloud the title and directions. Help students cut out the pictures and identify each as something you can read or not. Then help them glue the pictures into the basket.
Day 3	Read aloud the title and directions. Help students read the sentences. Then guide them to draw a circle around the word that correctly completes the sentence, and write the word on the line. (**Answers:** vowel, alphabet, consonant, author, character, story)
Day 4	Read aloud the title and directions. Help students identify the clues. Then guide them to find the word for each clue in the word list. Help them write the word into the puzzle.
Day 5	Read aloud the title and directions. **Say:** *Write an uppercase letter.* Allow students time to write. Then **say:** *Write a consonant.* (Allow responses.) **Say:** *Draw a picture of your favorite storybook character. Write his or her name next to the picture.* Afterward, meet individually with students to discuss their results. Use their responses to plan further instruction and review.

Provide a Real-World Example

◆ Display a book. **Say:** *This is a book. The title is* (title). Write **book** and **title** on the chart paper or the board. **Ask:** *Who is the author?* Write **author** on the chart paper. (Allow responses.) Point to the author's name and confirm their answer. **Say:** *A book has different parts.* Tap the front cover and **say:** *This is the front cover.* Flip the pages and **say:** *These are pages.* Turn it over and **say:** *This is the back cover.* Open to the title page and **say:** *This is the title page. Here's the title again.* Write the book parts on chart paper: **front cover**, **page**, **back cover**, **title page**.

◆ Open to a page in the book and magnify it if possible. Point to a word and **say:** *This is a word. A word is made up of letters.* Write **word** and **letter** on the chart paper. Now point to a vowel and **say:** *Some letters are vowels, such as* **a**, **e**, **i**, **o**, *and* **u**. Point to a consonant and **say:** *The other letters are consonants.* Then show uppercase and lowercase letters. Write **vowel**, **consonant**, **uppercase**, and **lowercase** on the chart paper. **Say:** *This week we will explore words that have to do with books, stories, and letters.*

Language Arts Words

book	word
title	letter
author	vowel
front cover	consonant
page	uppercase
back cover	lowercase
title page	

◆ Hand out the Day 1 activity page. **Say:** *Let's review the parts of a book.* Look at the book. Point to the title and remind students it is called a title. **Say:** *Let's trace and write the word* **title**. Ask students about their favorite book titles. Point to the picture and **say:** *He is the Ugly Duckling. The Ugly Duckling is a character in this fairy tale. Let's write and trace the word* **character**. Ask students about their favorite characters. Repeat with the remaining words.

Ugly Duckling

Listen to your teacher. Trace and write each word.

Bookstore

Bella loves to read. Cut out the things Bella can read and glue them into her basket.

book	cake	cartoon	dog	flower

hat	kite	magazine	newspaper	shirt

Complete-a-Sentence

Read each sentence. Draw a circle around the correct word to complete each sentence. Write it on the line.

1. The letter **o** is a _____.
   vowel   consonant

2. **A** is the first letter in the _____.
   story   alphabet

3. The letter **j** is a _____.
   vowel   consonant

4. A person who writes a book is the _____.
   author   character

5. A hero is an example of a _____.
   book   character

6. A fairy tale is a kind of _____.
   song   story

Crossword Puzzle

Look at each clue. Find the word in the word list that best describes each one. Write it into the puzzle.

author
character
hero
sentence
sign
title
uppercase
vowel

Clues

Down

1. B
2. Hans Christian Andersen
3. I like rainy days.

Across

4. Stop sign
5. u
6. Princess Fiona
7. Beauty and the Beast
8. Superman

Assessment

Listen to your teacher. Draw pictures to show your answer.

1

2

3

Overview Citizenship

Directions and Sample Answers for Activity Pages

Day 1	See "Provide a Real-World Example" below.
Day 2	Read aloud the title and directions. Help students identify each symbol.
Day 3	Read aloud the title and directions. Help students read the sentences. Then guide them to draw a circle around the word that correctly completes the sentence, and write the word on the line. (**Answers:** vote, bald eagle, freedom, national anthem, George Washington, citizen)
Day 4	Read aloud the title and directions. Help students cut out the words and choose words to glue onto the Bingo card. Then guide them to mark an X on the words you call out. Three in a row wins Bingo.
Day 5	Read aloud the directions. Allow time for students to complete the first task. Then **say:** *Draw a picture of a symbol of America. Label your picture.* Afterward, meet individually with students to discuss their results. Use their responses to plan further instruction and review.

Provide a Real-World Example

◆ Display a world map. Point to America. **Say:** *This is the United States of America. This is our country.* Write **United States of America** on chart paper or the board. Point to the U.S. flag and **say:** *This is our flag.* Write **flag** on the chart paper. **Ask:** *What do we say every day as we face the flag and put our hands on our hearts?* (Allow responses.) **Say:** *That's right! We pledge allegiance to the flag. That means that we are promising to be loyal, or true, to America.* Write **pledge allegiance** on the chart paper.

◆ Pass quarters with the bald eagle on them around the classroom. **Say:** *The bird is a bald eagle. The bald eagle is a symbol, or sign, of America.* Write **bald eagle** and **symbol** on the chart paper. Now display a picture of the Liberty Bell. **Say:** *The Liberty Bell is a symbol of America, too. The famous bell was rung to call the citizens, or people, of Pennsylvania together for the reading of the Declaration of Independence.* Write **Liberty Bell** and **citizens** on the chart paper. **Say:** *This week, we will explore words about America.*

Patriotic Words

United States of America

flag

pledge allegiance

bald eagle

symbol

Liberty Bell

citizens

◆ Hand out the Day 1 activity page. Point to the word **America** in the center of the word web inside the flag. **Say:** *When you think of America, many words come to mind. Trace and write* **America**. Draw attention to the bald eagle. **Say:** *The bald eagle is the national symbol for America. Trace and write* **bald eagle** *and* **symbol**. Draw attention to the balance scale. **Say:** *Justice means fair treatment. America's law, or rules, make sure that everyone is treated fairly. Trace and write* **justice** *and* **laws**. Now focus on the picture of Abraham Lincoln. **Say:** *America is a democracy. That means we vote for, or choose, our leaders. Americans voted for Abraham Lincoln as our sixteenth president. Trace and write* **democracy**, **leader**, *and* **vote**. Now focus on the Liberty Bell. **Say:** *The Liberty Bell is a symbol of freedom. Trace and write* **Liberty Bell** *and* **freedom**.

Name _____

I Pledge Allegiance . . .

Listen to your teacher. Trace and write each word.

bald eagle

_____

symbol

_____

justice

_____

laws

_____

America

_____

democracy

_____

leader

_____

vote

_____

Liberty Bell

_____

freedom

_____

Unit 9 • Everyday Vocabulary Intervention Activities Grade 2 • ©2011 Newmark Learning, LLC

Make-a-Match

Look at the pictures. Draw a line from each picture to a matching word or words.

America

bald eagle

Fourth of July

pledge allegiance

school

Complete-a-Sentence

Read each sentence. Draw a circle around the correct word or words that complete each sentence. Write the words on the lines.

1. We _____ for our leaders.

    vote   dance

2. The _____ is on a quarter.

    Liberty Bell   bald eagle

3. The Fourth of July celebrates America's _____.

    laws   freedom

4. At ball games, we sing the _____.

    national anthem   pledge of allegiance

5. _____ was America's first president.

    Martin Luther King Jr.   George Washington

6. Every adult _____ has the right to vote.

    citizen   bald eagle

Name _____

Patriotic Bingo

Cut out the words. Choose eight words to glue onto your Bingo card. Put an X on the word if the teacher calls it out. Three in a row wins Bingo!

	Free Space	

citizen	duty	election	flag	government	honesty
justice	law	leader	respect	responsibility	rules
volunteer	vote	nation	democracy	liberty	

Assessment

Read the questions. Draw a circle around the answer.

Which one is a symbol of America?

Fourth of July   **citizen**   **Liberty Bell**

Which do we pledge allegiance to?

bald eagle   **flag**   **Abraham Lincoln**

Which word means freedom?

citizen   **election**   **liberty**

What is the name of this country?

America   **George Washington**   **democracy**

Draw a symbol of the United States of America.

Overview Geography

Directions and Sample Answers for Activity Pages

Day 1	See "Provide a Real-World Example" below.
Day 2	Read aloud the title and directions. Tell students that Goldilocks just escaped the Three Bears' house and needs to get home. Guide them through the maze by reading aloud the route, step by step.
Day 3	Read aloud the title and directions. Help students cut out the words and pictures and mix them up. Show pairs how to lay out the pictures and words facedown in rows. Model turning over two cards to try to match a word and picture. If they match, explain to students that you keep them. If not, you return them to their spots facedown.
Day 4	Read aloud the title and directions. Help students identify the picture clues. Show them how to use the words in the word list to confirm their answers. Model how to write the words into the crossword puzzle.
Day 5	Read aloud the directions. **Say:** *Draw a map of your town. Draw a legend to identify the items in your map.* Afterward, meet individually with students to discuss their results. Use their responses to plan further instruction and review.

Provide a Real-World Example

◆ Display a map of your hometown. **Say:** *This is a map of our town.* Write **map** and **town** on chart paper or the board. Point to the legend and **say:** *This is a legend. A legend is a key that tells us what each symbol on the map means.* Write **legend**, **key**, and **symbol** on the chart paper. Point out examples from the legend, such as trees as a symbol for forest, wavy blue lines for body of water, and railroad tracks.

◆ Hand out the Day 1 activity page. Direct students' attention to the "Map Legend." Remind students that a legend says what each symbol on a map means. Review the symbols on this map legend. Then **say:** *Let's find the railroad on the map. When you find it, draw a circle around it.* Now **ask:** *Where is the park?* Allow students time to find it. Then guide them to draw a circle around the park. Continue with each symbol from the legend.

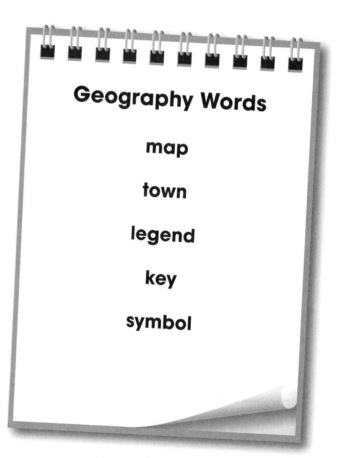

Geography Words

map

town

legend

key

symbol

Circle the Symbols

Find the symbols on the map.

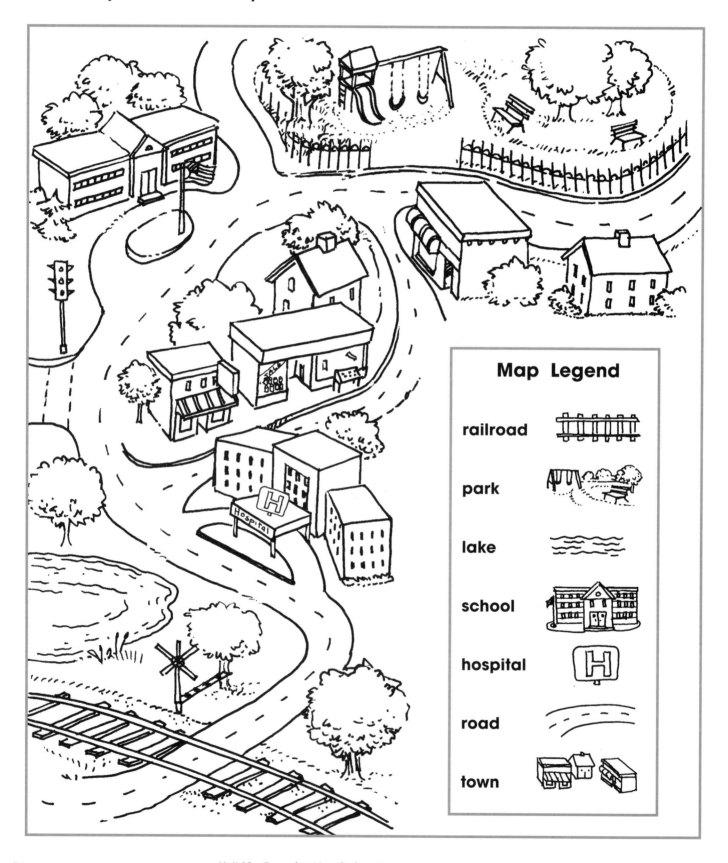

Map Legend

railroad

park

lake

school

hospital

road

town

Get Goldilocks Home

Help Goldilocks find her way home. Draw a line from one landmark to the next as follows.

First, Goldilocks runs away from the Three Bears' house and through the forest.

Next, Goldilocks walks on a road for one mile.

When she gets to the river, Goldilocks swims across.

Next, Goldilocks walks across the park.

After she climbs the hill, Goldilocks walks around the museum.

Finally, she is home.

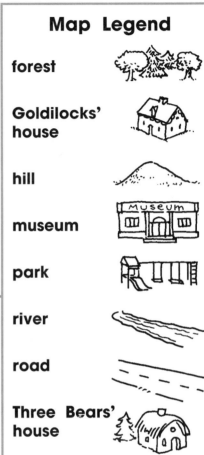

Map Legend

forest	
Goldilocks' house	
hill	
museum	
park	
river	
road	
Three Bears' house	

Name _____

Geography Concentration

Play with a partner. Cut out the pictures and words. Turn them over. Take turns trying to make a match.

forest	farm	fishing	hospital	mountain
railroad	road	village	stream	park

forest	farm	fishing	hospital	mountain
railroad	road	village	stream	park

  Unit 10 • Everyday Vocabulary Intervention Activities Grade 2 • ©2011 Newmark Learning, LLC

Name _____

Geography Crossword

Look at each picture clue. Find the word in the word list. Write it into the puzzle.

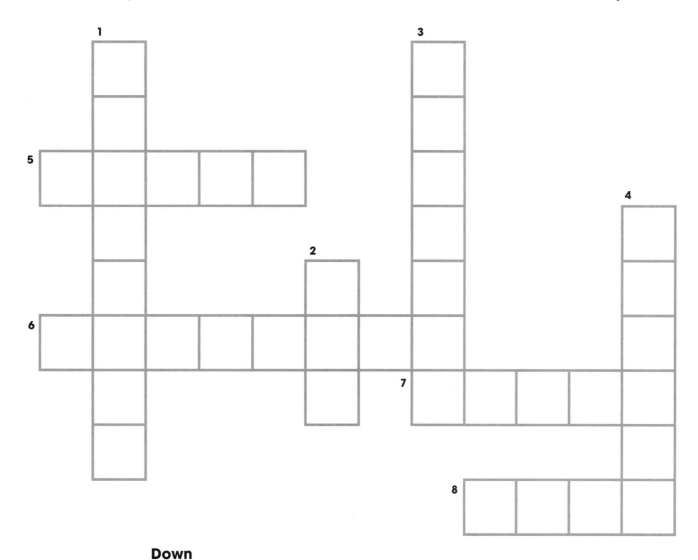

fishing
globe
legend
map
mountain
railroad
river
road

Down

1
2
3
4 Map Legend
forest
Goldilocks' house
hill
museum
park

Across

5
6
7
8

Name _____

Assessment

Draw a map of your town. Make a legend.

Map Legend

Overview Transportation

Directions and Sample Answers for Activity Pages

Day 1	See "Provide a Real-World Example" below.
Day 2	Read aloud the title and directions. Help students cut out the transportation words. Guide them to identify each as traveling by land, air, or sea and glue each one in the right place.
Day 3	Read aloud the title and directions. Guide students to identify each of the places: train station, bus station, shipping port, and airport. Then help them cut out each type of transportation and glue it in the correct space.
Day 4	Read aloud the title and directions. Help students read the sentences. Then guide them to draw a circle around the word or words that correctly complete the sentence, and to write the word(s) on the line. (**Answers:** motorcycle, skateboard, helicopter, shipping port, sign, bicycle)
Day 5	Read aloud the title and directions. Allow time for students to complete the task. Afterward, meet individually with students to discuss their results. Use their responses to plan further instruction and review.

Provide a Real-World Example

◆ Take the class outdoors. Point out a car in the parking lot or one driving on the road. **Say:** *A car is a type of transportation. Transportation is the way people get from one place to another.* Ask students to point out other forms of transportation that they see, such as a bus, bicycle, truck, or airplane. When you return to the classroom, write the word **transportation** on chart paper or the board. Then ask students to recall the types of transportation they saw outside and write their responses on the chart paper.

◆ Hand out the Day 1 activity page. **Say:** *Look at all the transportation!* Direct students' attention to the airplane. **Say:** *Look at the airplane. An airplane flies in the air.* Write the word **airplane** on the line. Draw students' attention to the bridge. **Say:** *A car, a truck, and a bus are driving over the bridge.* Write **bridge**, **car**, **truck**, and **bus** on the lines. Now **ask:** *What kind of transportation is in the water?* (Allow responses.) **Say:** *Yes, a ship takes people places by water.* Write **ship** on the line.

Transportation Words

transportation

airplane

bridge

car

truck

bus

ship

Name _____

On the Go

Write the transportation words on the lines.

airplane	truck	car
ship	bus	bridge

     Unit 11 • Everyday Vocabulary Intervention Activities Grade 2 • ©2011 Newmark Learning, LLC

Air, Land, or Sea?

Cut out the transportation. Glue each in Air, Land, or Sea.

Air 	Land 	Sea 

airplane

bicycle

bus

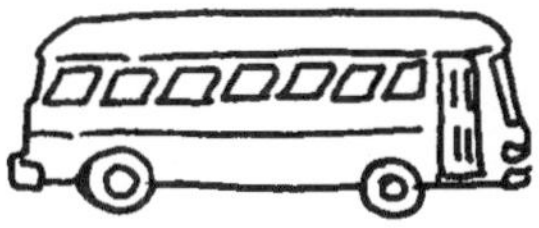

ferryboat

helicopter

skateboard

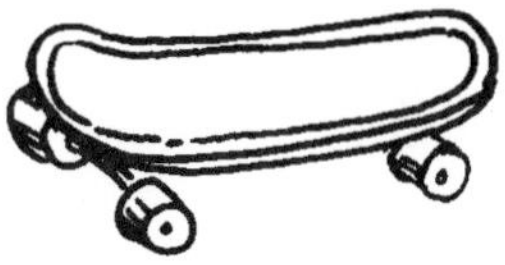

train

Transportation Locations

Cut out the pictures. Glue them where they belong.

Train Station	Bus Station	Shipping Port	Airport

airplane   **bus**   **ferryboat**   **train**

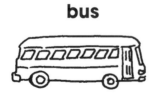

Complete-a-Sentence

Read each sentence. Draw a circle around the correct word or words that complete each sentence. Write the word or words on the line.

1. You must wear a helmet to ride a _____.

                 motorcycle   **train**

2. Your stand on a _____ to ride it.

       car   **skateboard**

3. A _____ flies in the air.

      car   **helicopter**

4. Ships come into a _____.

       shipping port   **train station**

5. Stop at a stop _____.

       bridge   **sign**

6. Riding a _____ is good exercise.

      bus   **bicycle**

Name _____

Assessment

Match the pictures to the words.

   **airplane**

   **bicycle**

   **bridge**

   **bus**

   **car**

   **ship**

   **skateboard**

   **train**

   Unit 11 • Everyday Vocabulary Intervention Activities Grade 2 • ©2011 Newmark Learning, LLC

Overview   Community

Directions and Sample Answers for Activity Pages

Day 1	See "Provide a Real-World Example" below.
Day 2	Read aloud the title and directions. Help students identify each picture as being rural, suburban, or urban, and draw a line to make a match. Then guide students to draw a picture of one of the three types of communities and label it.
Day 3	Read aloud the title and directions. Read aloud Willa's To-Do list. Help students use the list as a guide for Willa's walk in the community—her first stop is the first item on the list, her second stop is the second item, and so on. Model what to do by drawing a line from the first stop to the next.
Day 4	Read aloud the title and directions. Help students read the sentences. Then guide them to draw a circle around the word(s) that correctly complete(s) the sentence, and write the word(s) on the line. (an urban, rural, library, zoo, movie theater, an airport)
Day 5	Read aloud the directions. Allow time for students to complete the task. Afterward, meet individually with students to discuss their results. Use their responses to plan further instruction and review.

Provide a Real-World Example

◆ **Say:** *You go to school during the week. After school, you might go to the playground or the library. On the weekend, some of you go to the mall or see a film at the movie theater.* **Ask:** *What do all of these places have in common:* **school, playground, library, mall, movie theater**? (Allow responses.) Then **say:** *All of these places are in our community.* Write the word **community** on chart paper or the board. Write all the places listed above on the chart paper, too.

◆ **Say:** *We live in a(n) (urban, suburban, rural) community. But you will find schools, playgrounds, and libraries in all types of communities: urban, suburban, and rural.* Review the three kinds of communities. Write **urban**, **suburban**, and **rural** on the chart paper.

◆ Hand out the Day 1 activity page. **Say:** *Let's explore places in a community.* Direct students' attention to the pictures on the web. **Say:** *I see a tree and a bench. I know most communities have parks. I see the word* **park** *in the word list.* Write **park** on the line. Now focus on the zoo. **Say:** *Some communities have a zoo. I see* **zoo** *in the word list.* Write **zoo** on the line. Repeat with the other places on the concept web.

Community Words

school

playground

library

mall

community

movie theater

urban

suburban

rural

Name _____

Community Web

Identify and write the names of the places in a community.

bakery	houses	library	movie theater
park	playground	school	zoo

_____

_____

_____

Community

_____

_____

_____

_____

_____

Unit 12 • Everyday Vocabulary Intervention Activities Grade 2 • ©2011 Newmark Learning, LLC

Rural, Suburban, or Urban?

Draw a line to match each picture to its type of community. Then draw a picture of a rural, suburban, or urban community and label it.

skyscrapers

rural

houses

urban

farm

suburban

Wonderville

Willa has a lot to do in town today. Read her To-Do list. Then draw a line to show Willa's route through Wonderville.

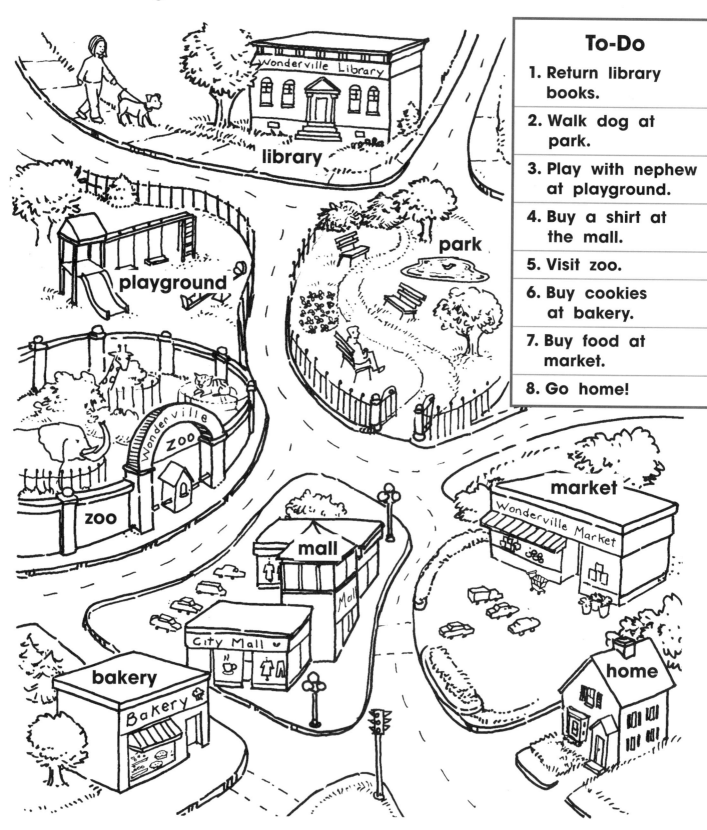

To-Do
1. Return library books.
2. Walk dog at park.
3. Play with nephew at playground.
4. Buy a shirt at the mall.
5. Visit zoo.
6. Buy cookies at bakery.
7. Buy food at market.
8. Go home!

Complete-a-Sentence

Read each sentence. Draw a circle around the correct word or words that complete each sentence. Write the word or words on the line.

1. Skyscrapers are in _____ community.

    an urban   a suburban

2. Farms are in a _____ community.

    suburban   rural

3. You borrow books from a _____.

    zoo   library

4. Do not feed the animals at a _____.

    zoo   train station

5. People eat popcorn at a _____.

    school   movie theater

6. Airplanes fly into _____.

    an airport   a bus station

Assessment

Draw a picture of your community. Include at least five places listed in the word list. Label the places in your picture.

airport	bakery	farm	houses	library	market	movie theater
park	playground	school	shopping mall	skyscraper	zoo	

Overview   Life Science: Living and Nonliving Things

Directions and Sample Answers for Activity Pages

Day 1	See "Provide a Real-World Example" below.
Day 2	Read aloud the title and directions. Help students cut out the pictures and identify each as living or nonliving. Then guide them to glue living things in the leaf and nonliving things in the rock. (**Living:** bear, bee, bird, butterfly, pine tree, ant; **Nonliving:** air, ice, fossil, sand, water)
Day 3	Read aloud the title and directions. Read aloud the words in the word list. Help students write the words on the proper lines to label the plant diagram.
Day 4	Read aloud the title and directions. Remind students that plants and animals are living things. Explain that all living things need certain other things to live; for example, animals need food. Help students cut out the words and guide them to glue the animal needs on the animal side, the plant needs on the plant side, and things they both need in the overlapping section. (**Plant Needs:** soil, sunlight; **Animal Needs:** shelter; **Both:** food, air, water, space)
Day 5	Read aloud the directions. Allow time for students to complete the first task. Then read the directions for the second task. After students complete the second task, meet individually with students to discuss their results. Use their responses to plan further instruction and review.

Provide a Real-World Example

◆ Invite a student to the front of the class. **Say:** *You are a living thing.* Point out the window to a tree and **say:** *A tree is a living thing, too. All plants and animals are living things.* Write **living things** on chart paper or the board. Beneath it, write **tree**, **plants**, and **animals**. Now hold up a glass of water. **Ask:** *Is water a living thing?* (Allow responses.) **Say:** *Water is a nonliving thing.* Point to a rock outside and **say:** *A rock is a nonliving thing, too.* Write **nonliving things** on the chart paper. Beneath it write **water** and **rock**.

◆ Hand out the Day 1 activity page. **Say:** *Let's explore the living and nonliving things in a forest.* Direct students' attention to the butterfly. **Say:** *A butterfly is a living thing. Trace and write* **butterfly**. **Ask:** *What is another living thing you see?* (Allow responses.) After several students respond, invite them to trace and write those words. Now direct students' attention to the forest floor. **Say:** *This is soil. Soil is a nonliving thing. Trace and write the word* **soil**. Encourage students to identify other nonliving things. Review each labeled item in the forest, guiding students to trace and write each word. If time allows, students may color in the picture.

Life Science Words

living things

tree

plants

animals

nonliving things

water

rock

Fun in the Forest

Trace and write the names of living and nonliving things in the forest.

Name _____

Living or Nonliving?

Cut out the pictures. Glue the living things inside the leaf. Glue the nonliving things inside the rock.

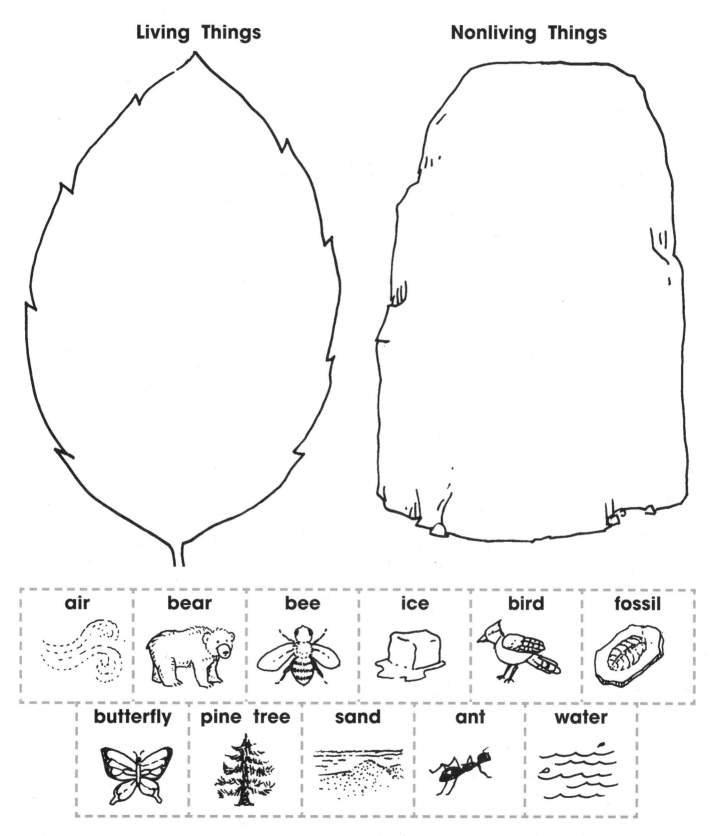

Living Things

Nonliving Things

air	bear	bee	ice	bird	fossil

butterfly	pine tree	sand	ant	water

Label-a-Plant

Label the plant by using the words in the word list and writing them on the proper line.

bud	flower	leaf	soil	stem

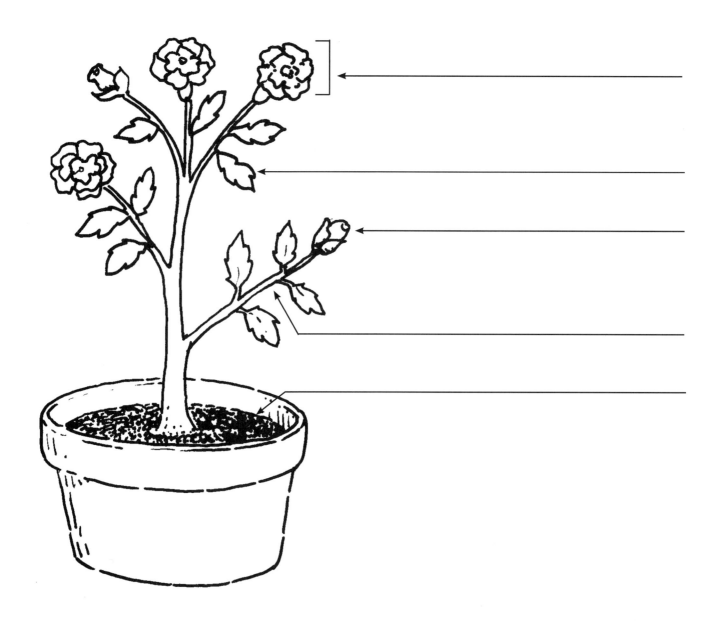

Plant and Animal Needs

Cut out the words. Identify each word as an animal need, a plant need, or both. Glue it in the correct place.

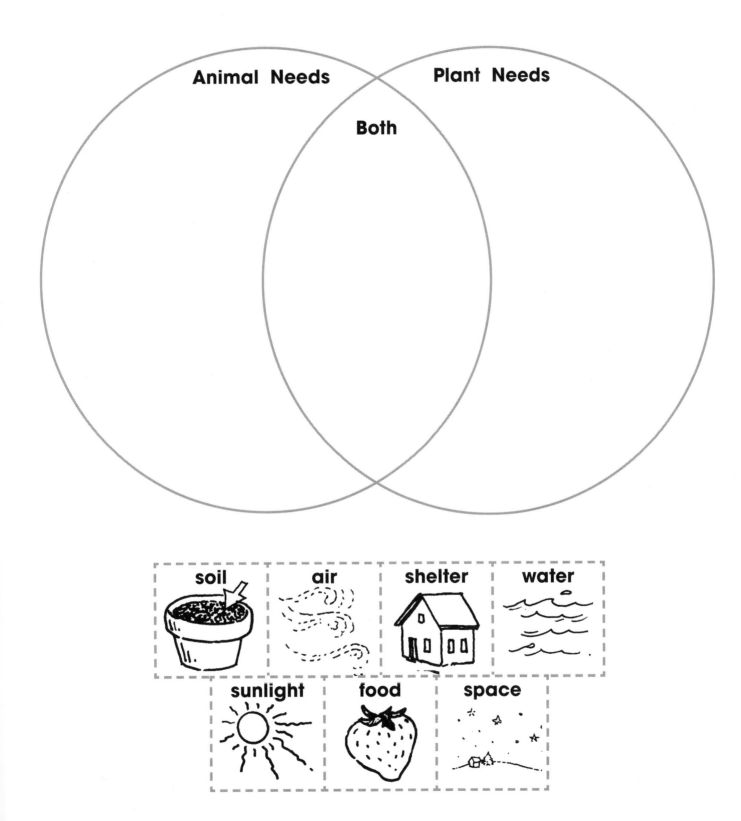

Assessment

Draw a line to make a match between pictures and words.

bear

bird

leaf

pine tree

rocks

water

Draw a living thing. Label it. Draw and label something that this living thing needs
to survive.

Living thing	Living thing needs . . .

_____   _____

Overview Life Science: Human Body

● ●

Directions and Sample Answers for Activity Pages

Day 1	See "Provide a Real-World Example" below.
Day 2	Read aloud the title and directions. Help students identify each body part. Guide them to draw a line from each body part to how we use it. (tongue/taste, nose/smell, ear/hear, eye/see, hand/feel)
Day 3	Read aloud the title and directions. Explain that a food pyramid tells how much and what kind of food to eat daily. Help students cut out the pictures of food and glue them into the correct part of the food pyramid. (**grains:** bread; **vegetables:** carrot, lettuce; **fruits:** apple, banana; **milk:** cheese, yogurt; **meat:** chicken, fish)
Day 4	Read aloud the title and directions. Help students read each sentence. Guide them to draw a circle around the word that correctly completes the sentence and to write it on the line. (body, heart, sleep, energy, lungs, joints, fruit)
Day 5	Read aloud the directions. Allow time for students to complete the tasks. Afterward, meet individually with students to discuss their results. Use their responses to plan further instruction and review. (eyes, exercise, fish, hear, lungs)

Provide a Real-World Example

◆ Ask students to locate their different body parts, such as head, shoulders, knees, toes, eyes, ears, mouth, and nose. Allow time for them to show you each part.

◆ Afterward, invite students to play the singing game "Head, Shoulders, Knees, and Toes." Sing the song and model the movements as students follow along:
Head, shoulders, knees and toes, knees and toes.
Head, shoulders, knees and toes, knees and toes.
Eyes and ears and mouth and nose,
Head, shoulders, knees and toes, knees and toes.

◆ After you play the game, write these words on chart paper or the board: **head, shoulders, knees, toes, eyes, ears, mouth, nose.**

◆ **Say:** *This week we will explore body words and words about healthy living.*

◆ Hand out the Day 1 activity page. Invite students to help you label the body parts. Direct their attention to the head. **Say:** *This is the head. Let's find the word* **head** *in the word list. I see it! Now write it on the line next to the* **head**. **Ask:** *Where is the arm?* (Allow responses.) Then guide them to find **arm** in the word list and write it on the line. Repeat with the rest of the body parts.

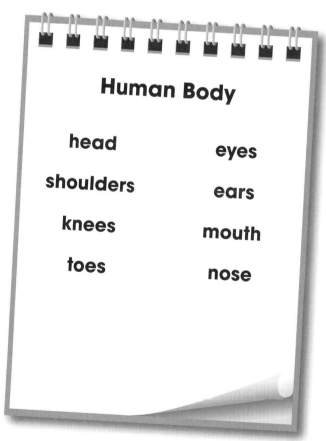

Human Body

head   eyes

shoulders   ears

knees   mouth

toes   nose

Label-a-Body

Label the body parts. Use the words in the word list to help you.

arm	ear	elbow	eye	foot	hand	head	hip
knee	leg	mouth	neck	nose	shoulder	stomach	

The Five Senses

Draw a line from each body part to what you use it for.

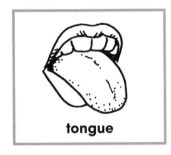
tongue

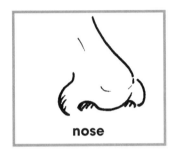
nose

ear

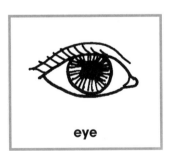
eye

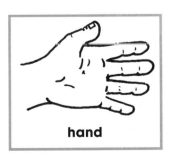
hand

see

feel

taste

hear

smell

Food Pyramid

Cut out the foods. Glue each picture in the correct part of the food pyramid.

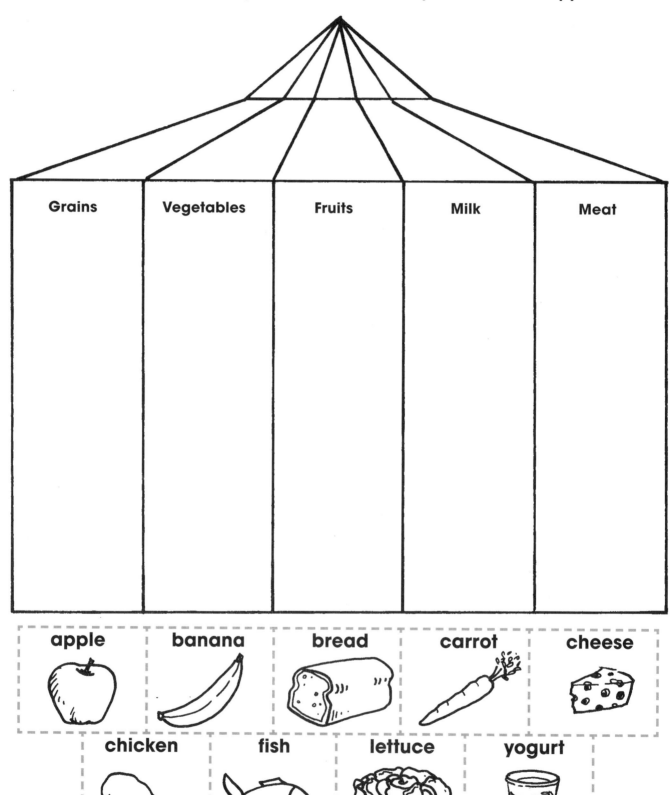

Complete-a-Sentence

Read each sentence. Draw a circle around the word that correctly completes each sentence. Write the word on the line.

Exercise is good for your _____.

                           body   **fingernails**

Your _____ pumps blood around your body.

       stomach   **heart**

Children need at least 10 hours of _____ each night.

                                  TV   **sleep**

Food gives you _____.

                      energy   **exercise**

We breathe air through our _____.

                             heart   **lungs**

Knees and elbows are examples of _____.

                         joints   **vegetables**

Apples and grapes are _____.

                   meat   **fruit**

Assessment

Read each question. Draw a circle around the correct answer.

Which lets you see?

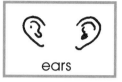 ears   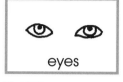 eyes

Which keeps your heart strong?

 exercise    sleep

Which is good for your body?

 fish    cookie

What do your ears help you do?

 smell    hear

Which lets you breathe?

 lungs    legs

Draw a picture of your favorite healthy food. Label it.

Favorite Healthy Food

Draw a picture of you doing exercise. Label it.

Exercise

Overview   Earth Science

Directions and Sample Answers for Activity Pages

Day 1	See "Provide a Real-World Example" below.
Day 2	Read aloud the title and directions. Help students identify each clue. Guide them to find the word for each clue in the word list. Help them write the clue into the puzzle.
Day 3	Read aloud the title and directions. Explain to students that erosion occurs when Earth wears away because of water, wind, or ice. Help students cut out the pictures of the erosion words and glue them with the matching pictures on the concept web.
Day 4	Write the Bingo words on scraps of paper and put them in a container. Read aloud the title and directions. Pick words and read them aloud as you write them on the board. Remind them to say "Bingo" when they have three in a row.
Day 5	Read aloud the directions. Allow time for students to complete the task. Afterward, meet individually with students to discuss their results. Use their responses to plan further instruction and review. (Answers: Earth, volcanoes, heat, clouds, wind)

Provide a Real-World Example

◆ **Ask:** *What planet do we live on?* (Allow responses.) **Say:** *Yes! We live on Earth. Earth and seven other planets are in space. Stars are in space, too.* Write **planet**, **Earth**, **space**, and **stars** on chart paper or the board.

◆ Take the class outside and **say:** *We may not be able to see the other planets from Earth, but there are many cool things right here on our planet.* Pick up a handful of soil and rocks and **say:** *Earth has soil and rocks that make up mountains. We also have bodies of water, including ponds, lakes, and oceans.*

◆ Upon returning to the classroom, write the words discussed outside on the chart paper: **soil**, **rocks**, **mountains**, **ponds**, **lakes**, **oceans**.

◆ Hand out the Day 1 activity page. **Say:** *There is a limited amount of water on Earth. And that same water keeps moving around and around. That movement is called the water cycle.* Trace and write **water cycle**. *Let's look at the water cycle together.* Draw students' attention to Step 1. **Say:** *First, the sun heats up water in ponds, lakes, and oceans. The heat causes water to evaporate, or turn*

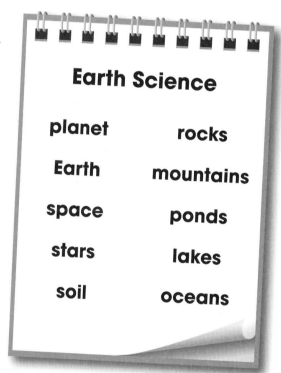

Earth Science

planet	rocks
Earth	mountains
space	ponds
stars	lakes
soil	oceans

into vapor. Trace and write **evaporate**. *The vapor leaves the water and goes into the air.* Focus attention on Step 2. **Say:** *The air makes the vapor cold and it becomes water again. The water makes clouds.* Trace and write **clouds**. Move on to Step 3. **Say:** *When the clouds get very heavy with water, the water falls to Earth as rain.* Trace and write **rain**. Direct attention to the last step. **Say:** *The rain falls back into the ponds, lakes, and oceans and onto the land. Some of that rain soaks into the earth, and some is runoff. In other words, it runs over the ground and back into the ponds, lakes, and oceans. The water cycle begins again.* Trace and write **runoff**.

Water Goes Around and Around and Around

Listen to your teacher. Trace and write the steps in the water cycle.

water cycle _____

clouds

rain

evaporate

_____

runoff _____

Name _____

Earth Science Crossword

Look at the picture clues. Find the word in the word list. Fill in the crossword puzzle.

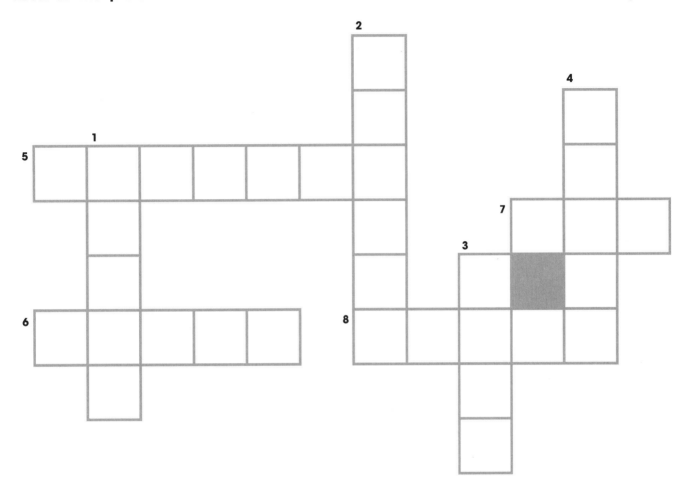

| clouds |
| Earth |
| ice |
| ocean |
| rain |
| rocks |
| stars |
| volcano |

Erosion Web

Cut out the words at the bottom of the page. Glue them under the correct picture.

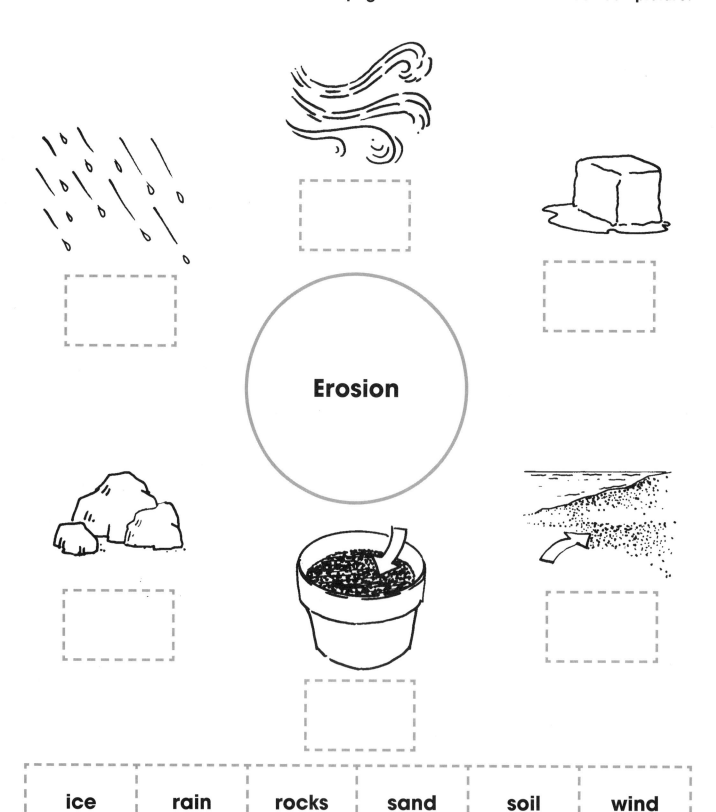

| ice | rain | rocks | sand | soil | wind |

Bingo!

Cut out the words. Glue them into the Bingo card. Play Bingo!

	Free Space	

Earth	space	stars	fossils
mountains	clouds	ponds	water cycle
ice	rocks	sand	soil

Assessment

Read each question. Draw a circle around the correct answer.

Which is a planet?

stars

Earth

Which erupts?

volcano

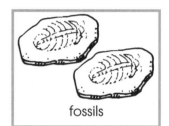
fossils

What makes water evaporate?

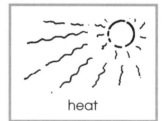
heat

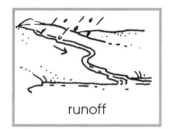
runoff

Where does rain fall from?

lake

clouds

What is one cause of erosion?

stars

wind

Overview   Physical Science

Directions and Sample Answers for Activity Pages

Day 1	See "Provide a Real-World Example" below.
Day 2	Read aloud the title and directions. Help students cut out the pictures. Guide students to identify each as showing a push or a pull and glue them in the correct column.
Day 3	Read aloud the title and directions. Help students identify the pictures and draw a line to the type of simple machine it is. (well/pulley, roller coaster/inclined plane, bicycle/wheel, seesaw/lever, doorstop/wedge)
Day 4	Read aloud the title and directions. Guide students to find the correct simple machine in each row and draw a circle around it. (pulley/crane, wedge/ax, lever/can opener, wheel/wheelchair, inclined plane/slide)
Day 5	Read aloud the directions. Allow time for students to complete the task. Afterward, meet individually with students to discuss their results. Use their responses to plan further instruction and review.

Provide a Real-World Example

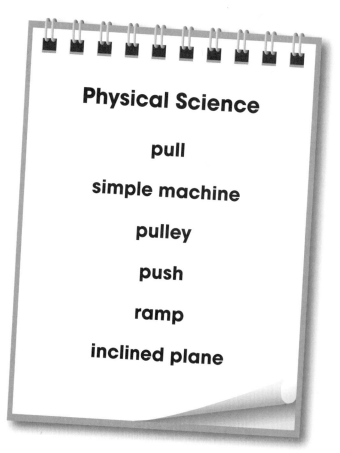

Physical Science

pull

simple machine

pulley

push

ramp

inclined plane

◆ Pull down a shade. Pull a chair toward you. **Say:** *I pulled down the shade. I pulled a chair.* Write **pull** on chart paper. **Say:** *We pull things all day long. What is something else you pull?* (Allow responses.)

◆ Take students to see the flagpole at your school. Point out the pulley and **say:** *This is a pulley. A pulley is a simple machine that makes lifting things easier.* Back in the classroom, write **simple machine** and **pulley** on the chart paper.

◆ Now demonstrate pushing. Push a stack of books; push a chair. Display a picture of a wheelchair on a ramp. **Say:** *A ramp is a simple machine, too. It makes pushing uphill easier. A ramp is also called an inclined plane.* Write **push**, **ramp**, and **inclined plane** on the chart paper.

◆ Hand out the Day 1 activity page. **Say:** *Playgrounds are full of simple machines!* Direct attention to the flagpole. **Say:** *The rope and pulley make lifting the flag easier.* Trace and write **rope** and **pulley**. **Say:** *The wheels make it easy for the boy to move things in his wagon.* Trace and write **wheel**. **Say:** *A seesaw is a lever, another simple machine. The lever makes it easier for friends to lift each other.* Trace and write **lever**. **Say:** *The slide is an inclined plane. The slanting surface helps a child come down slow and safe. The ladder is also an inclined plane. It helps a child get to the top more easily.* Trace and write **inclined plane**.

Simple Machines at the Playground

Listen to your teacher. Trace and write the names of the simple machines.

Push or Pull?

Cut out the pictures. Glue the pictures that show pushing in the "Push" column.
Glue the pictures that show pulling in the "Pull" column.

Push	Pull

Machine Match-Up

Match the pictures to the simple machines by drawing a line.

well

pulley

rollercoaster

wedge

bicycle

lever

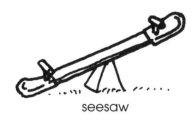

seesaw

wheel

door stop

inclined plane

Which Machine Is It?

Read the name of each simple machine. Draw a circle around the picture that shows that type of simple machine.

pulley

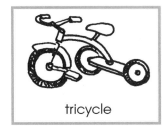
tricycle

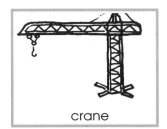
crane

wedge

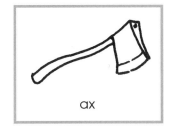
ax

screw

lever

can opener

water well

wheel

hammer

wheelchair

inclined plane

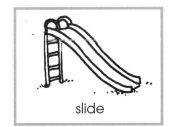
slide

doorknob

Assessment

Select one of the simple machines in the word list. Draw an example of you using the simple tool. Write the name of the tool and the type of simple machine.

inclined plane   lever   pulley   wedge   wheel

_____   _____

Overview Addition and Subtraction

Directions and Sample Answers for Activity Pages

Day 1	See "Provide a Real-World Example" below.
Day 2	Read aloud the title and directions. Help students cut out the pictures and numerals and place them facedown on a table. Guide them to match a picture with a numeral. If no match is made, show them how to return the pictures and numerals to the facedown position.
Day 3	Read aloud the title and directions. Help students add the two sets of scoops in each equation. Guide them to draw the total scoops on each cone. Invite students to come up with their own ice cream math problem for a classmate to solve.
Day 4	Read aloud the title and directions. Help students read each sentence. Guide them to draw a circle around the word that correctly completes the sentence and write it on the line. (sum, difference, minus, plus, subtract, add)
Day 5	Read aloud the directions. Allow time for students to complete the task. Afterward, meet individually with students to discuss their results. Use their responses to plan further instruction and review.

Provide a Real-World Example

◆ Hold up one pencil. **Say:** *I have one pencil.* In your other hand, hold up three more pencils. **Say:** *I found three more pencils. One pencil* (hold up the one-pencil hand) *plus three pencils* (hold up the three-pencil hand) *is a total of four pencils.* Count out the four pencils to model how three plus one is four. Write **one**, **three**, **plus**, and **total** on chart paper or the board.

◆ Invite a student to the front of the classroom. Give the student one of your four pencils as you **say:** *I give away, or subtract, one pencil. I had four pencils before. Now I have three pencils. The difference between four pencils and three pencils is one pencil.* Write **four**, **subtract**, and **difference** on the chart paper.

◆ Hand out the Day 1 activity page. **Say:** *The boy picked ten apples. His friend picked eight more apples.* **Ask:** *If they* **add** *their apples together, what is the* **sum**, *or total number of apples?* (Allow responses.) Then **say:** *Ten* **plus** *eight is eighteen.* Write the numeral 18. Trace the words **add**, **plus**, and **sum**. Now **say:** *Ellie has nine flowers. Her sister Abby has just seven flowers.* **Ask:** *What is the difference between the numbers of flowers each sister has?* (Allow responses.) Then **say:** *Nine* **minus** *seven is two. Ellie has two more flowers than Abby.* Write the numeral 2 and trace the words **subtract**, **minus**, and **difference**.

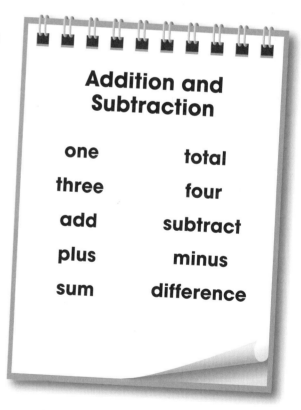

Addition and Subtraction

one	**total**
three	**four**
add	**subtract**
plus	**minus**
sum	**difference**

Add 'em, Subtract 'em

Listen to your teacher. Write the answers. Trace the words.

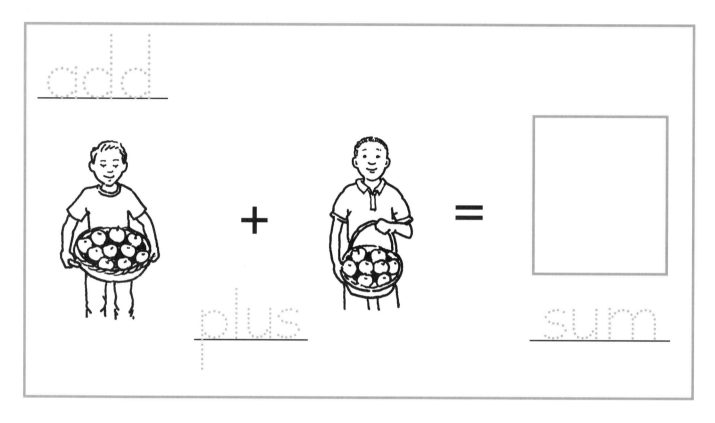

Concentration

Cut out the pictures and numerals. Place them facedown. Take turns trying
to match the pictures with the numerals.

Name _____

What's the Scoop?

Do the math. Draw the total number of scoops.

 **+**   **=**

 **—**  **=**

 **—** **=**

 **+**  **=**

Make up an ice cream addition or subtraction problem. Invite a partner to solve it.

 **=**

Unit 17 • Everyday Vocabulary Intervention Activities Grade 2 • ©2011 Newmark Learning, LLC

Complete-a-Sentence

Read each sentence. Draw a circle around the word that correctly completes each sentence. Write the word on the line.

1. The _____ of 2 and 4 is 6.

          sum   **minus**

2. The _____ between 9 and 5 is 4.

          total   **difference**

3. 10 cookies _____ 3 cookies is 7 cookies

          plus   **minus**

4. 16 hearts _____ 4 hearts is 20 hearts.

          plus   **minus**

5. To find the difference, you _____.

          subtract   **add**

6. To find the total, you _____.

          subtract   **add**

Name _____

Assessment

Draw a line to make a match.

+	difference
7	eighteen
18	minus
11 — 7 = (4)	seven
—	sum
0	three
20	twenty
8 + 2 = (10)	zero
5	plus
3	five

Unit 17 • Everyday Vocabulary Intervention Activities Grade 2 • ©2011 Newmark Learning, LLC

Overview   Whole Numbers and Money

Directions and Sample Answers for Activity Pages

Day 1	See "Provide a Real-World Example" below.
Day 2	Read aloud the title and directions. Help students cut out, identify, and group coins. Guide students to glue coin groups in separate jars. Help them count the amount in each jar. Remind them to draw a circle around the jar with the most amount of money and a square around the jar with the least. (Most: dimes; Least: quarters)
Day 3	Read aloud the title and directions. Read aloud the sentences. Guide students to write the missing numerals on the line to complete the math sentence.
Day 4	Read aloud the title and directions. Help students read each sentence. Guide them to use the word list to find the missing phrase. (equal to, less than, less than, more than, equal to)
Day 5	Read aloud the directions. Allow time for students to complete both tasks. Afterward, meet individually with students to discuss their results. Use their responses to plan further instruction and review.

Provide a Real-World Example

◆ Pass around pennies, nickels, dimes, and quarters. On an overhead or whiteboard, display a penny. **Say:** *A penny is equal to one cent.* Write **penny** and **one cent** on chart paper or the board. Now display five pennies and count them. **Say:** *Five pennies equal five cents.* Display a nickel next to the five pennies. **Say:** *A nickel is equal to five pennies. A nickel is five cents.* Write **nickel** and **equal to** on the chart paper. Now display a dime. **Say:** *A dime is equal to ten cents. A dime is greater than a nickel.* Write **dime** and **greater than** on the chart paper. Display three dimes. **Ask:** *What are the three dimes equal to?* Count by tens as you point to each dime. **Say:** *Ten, twenty, thirty. Three dimes are equal to thirty cents.*

◆ Display a quarter. **Say:** *A quarter is twenty-five cents.* **Say:** *A dime is less than a quarter.* Write **quarter** and **less than** on the chart paper. **Say:** *A nickel is less than a quarter, too. Remember a nickel is five cents. Let's count how many nickels are equal to a quarter.* Display one nickel at a time as you count by fives. **Say:** *Five nickels equal one quarter.*

◆ Hand out the Day 1 activity page. **Say:** *Let's review the names and values of each coin.* Focus attention on the penny. **Say:** *A penny is equal to one cent.* Find **penny** in the word list. Write it on the line. Ask students to put their finger on the nickel. Have them find the word **nickel** and write it on the line. Repeat with **dime** and **quarter**. When students are done writing, read the sentence *A penny is less than a dime.* Have students trace the words **less than**. Then **say:** *A dime is more than a nickel.* Trace the words **more than**. Finally, **say:** *A quarter is equal to two dimes and one nickel.* Trace the words **equal to**.

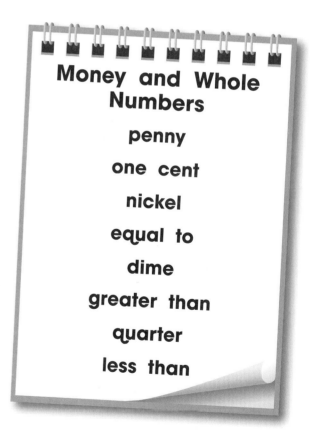

Money and Whole Numbers

penny

one cent

nickel

equal to

dime

greater than

quarter

less than

Money Fun

Listen to your teacher. Write the words.

| dime | nickel | penny | quarter |

_____   _____   _____   _____

penny   **nickel**   **dime**   **quarter**

Listen to your teacher. Write the words.

A is *less than* a .
penny   dime

A  is *more than* a .
dime   nickel

A  is *equal to* two  and one .
quarter   dimes   nickel

Counting Coins

Cut out the coins. Group them by type and glue them in jars. Draw a circle around the jar with the greatest amount of money. Draw a rectangle around the jar with the least amount of money.

nickel   dime   quarter

Story Problems

Read each story problem. Complete the math sentence that solves the problem by writing the missing numerals.

Jordan has twenty dollars. Olivia has three less dollars than Jordan. How many dollars does Olivia have?

$$20 - \underline{\hspace{3cm}} = 17 \text{ dollars}$$

Gumballs cost ten cents. Lollipops cost thirty cents. If you wanted to buy one gumball and one lollipop, how much would they cost?

$$10 + \underline{\hspace{3cm}} = 40 \text{ cents}$$

Alex has 40 baseball cards. Ali has five more baseball cards than Alex. How many baseball cards does Ali have?

$$40 + \underline{\hspace{3cm}} = 45 \text{ baseball cards}$$

Maria saved one hundred dollars. Anna saved five less dollars than Maria. How many dollars did Anna save?

$$\underline{\hspace{3cm}} - 5 = 95 \text{ dollars}$$

More Than, Less Than, or Equal To

Complete each math sentence using one of the phrases in the word list.

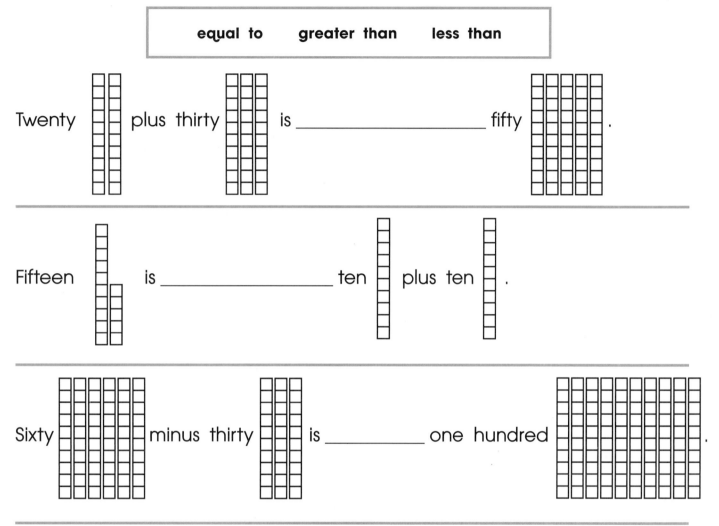

| equal to | greater than | less than |

Twenty [ ] plus thirty [ ] is _____ fifty [ ] .

Fifteen [ ] is _____ ten [ ] plus ten [ ] .

Sixty [ ] minus thirty [ ] is _____ one hundred [ ] .

Five [ ] plus ten [ ] is _____ twelve [ ] .

Eighty [ ] is _____ forty [ ] plus forty [ ] .

Assessment

Draw a line to match the coins with their amounts.

nickel

quarter

penny

dime

twenty-five cents

ten cents

five cents

one cent

Listen to your teacher read the prompts. Write your answers on the lines.

Write a number greater than seventy. _____

Write a number equal to ten plus ten. _____

Write a number less than thirty. _____

Overview   Shapes, Numbers, and Patterns

Directions and Sample Answers for Activity Pages

Day 1	See "Provide a Real-World Example" below.
Day 2	Read aloud the title and directions. Model the first example. Point out that the first shape is a square. Count the sides and angles aloud and show students where to write the names and numbers.
Day 3	Read aloud the title and directions. Help students cut out the kites. Explain that a pattern repeats shapes, colors, numbers, etc. Guide students to see that the first pattern is one, two, one, two, one, etc. Help them glue the set of two kites to continue the pattern.
Day 4	Read aloud the title and directions. Help students read each sentence. Review the position words as necessary, including **before**, **after**, **between**, **first**, and **next**. (five, three, four, zero, ten)
Day 5	Read aloud the directions. Allow time for students to complete the first task. Then **say:** *Draw the next shape in this pattern: circle, circle, triangle, circle, circle, triangle, circle, circle . . .* Afterward, meet individually with students to discuss their results. Use their responses to plan further instruction and review.

Provide a Real-World Example

◆ Hold up a book and **ask:** *What shape is this book?* (Allow responses.) Then **say:** *Yes. A book is a rectangle.* Write **shape** and **rectangle** on chart paper or the board. **Say:** *Let's count how many sides are on a rectangle.* Count each side as you point to it. **Say:** *A rectangle has four sides.* Write **four** and **sides** on the chart paper. **Say:** *A rectangle also has angles. An angle is where two sides come together.* Point to an angle on the book. **Say:** *A rectangle has four angles.* Count each angle as you point to it. Write **angles** on the chart paper.

◆ Point to the wall clock. **Ask:** *What shape is the clock?* **Say:** *Yes, the clock is a circle.* Write **circle** on the chart paper. Then **ask:** *How many sides does a circle have?* (Allow responses.) Then **say:** *A circle has zero sides.* Write **zero** on the chart paper.

◆ Hand out the Day 1 activity page. **Say:** *We can see signs and signals all around our community. Knowing the shapes of signs and signals helps us follow the rules of the road and stay safe.* Point out the yield sign. **Say:** *This is a yield sign. It tells drivers to slow down at an intersection. It is a **triangle**. Let's find the word **triangle** in the word list and write it on the line.*

◆ Point out the stop sign. **Say:** *Let's count the sides on a stop sign.* Count the sides together. Then **say:** *A stop sign has eight sides. An eight-sided shape is called an octagon.* Help students find the word **octagon** in the word list and write it on the line. Now point out the circles in the traffic light. Have students find and write **circle**. Repeat with the rest of the signs and signals.

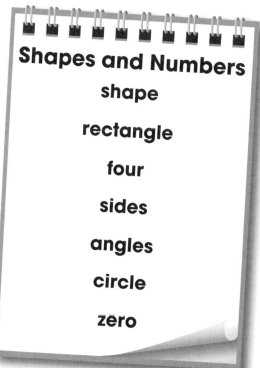

Shapes and Numbers

shape

rectangle

four

sides

angles

circle

zero

Signs and Shapes

Listen to your teacher. Write the words.

circle	diamond	octagon	pentagon
rectangle	square	triangle	

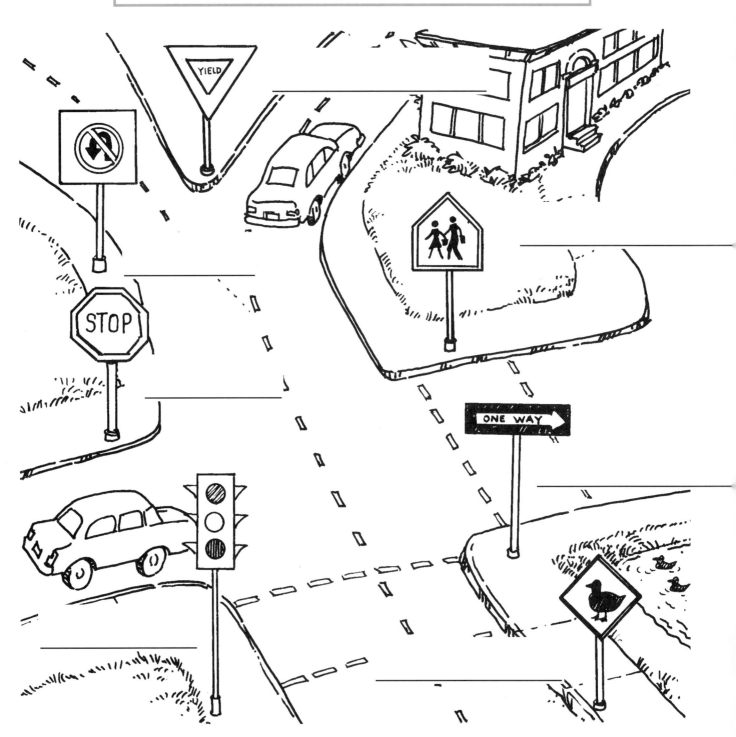

Shape ID

Look at the example. Complete the chart.

| circle | hexagon | octagon | rectangle |
| rhombus | square | triangle | |

Shape	Shape Name	Sides	Angles

Finish the Pattern

Cut out the kite sets. Glue the set that continues each pattern at the end of each row.

one kite	two kites	one kite	two kites	one kite

_____

one kite	one kite	four kites	one kite	one kite

_____

one kite	two kites	three kites	one kite	two kites

_____

two kites	three kites	four kites

Number Lines

Read each question. Look at the number line. Answer the question.

Which number comes just before six? _____

Which number comes just after two? _____

Which number is between three and five? _____

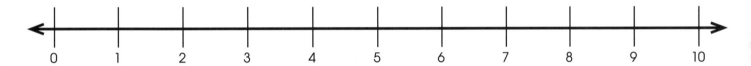

Which is the first number in this number line? _____

Which number comes next? _____

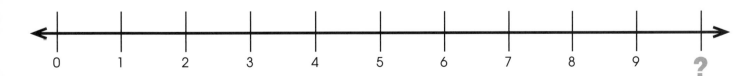

Assessment

Draw a line to match each shape with its name. Draw a circle around a shape with zero sides. Color in a shape with three angles.

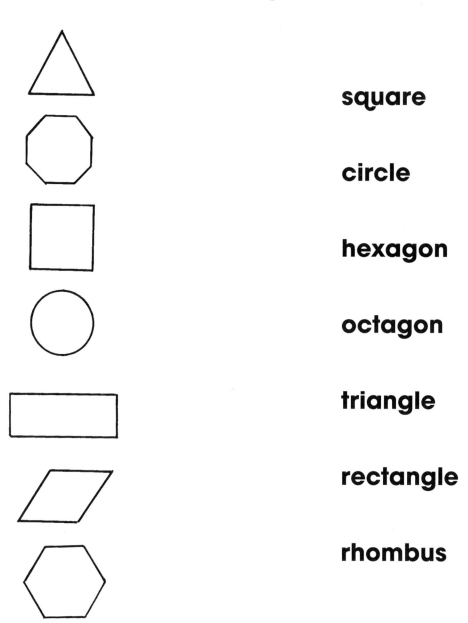

square

circle

hexagon

octagon

triangle

rectangle

rhombus

Listen to your teacher. Draw the next shape in the pattern.

Overview   Measurement

• •

Directions and Sample Answers for Activity Pages

Day 1	See "Provide a Real-World Example" below.
Day 2	Read aloud the title and directions. Help students cut out the words. Guide students to identify each word as being a clock or calendar measurement and glue it under the correct picture. (**Clock:** hour, minute, second; **Calendar:** day, month, week, year)
Day 3	Read aloud the title and directions. Divide the class into pairs. Model how to play with a volunteer. Encourage students to say aloud which item is longer. For example, if the cards come up as tree and man, **say:** *A tree is longer than a man.* Remind students to play again, this time with the shorter picture winning the hands.
Day 4	Read aloud the title and directions. Help students read each sentence and identify which phrase correctly completes the sentence.
Day 5	Read aloud the directions. Allow time for students to complete the tasks. Afterward, meet individually with students to discuss their results. Use their responses to plan further instruction and review.

Provide a Real-World Example

◆ Hold up a ruler. Ask students what it is and what we use it for. (Allow responses.) Then **say:** *This is a ruler. It has numbers on it. We use rulers to measure. When we measure how long something is, we find out its length.* Measure how tall a book is. **Say:** *The book has a length of (X) inches.* **Say:** *We can also measure how wide something is, or its width.* Demonstrate how to measure the width of the book. Then **say:** *The book has a width of (X) inches.* Write **ruler**, **measure**, **length**, and **width** on chart paper or the board.

◆ **Ask:** *What does the doctor measure at your check-up?* (Allow responses.) Then **say:** *Your doctor measures your height, or how tall you are, and your weight, or how heavy you are.* Write **height** and **weight** on the chart paper. **Say:** *Each year your weight is greater than the year before. And your length is longer than the year before.* Write, **greater than**, **longer than**, and **year** on the chart paper.

◆ Hand out the Day 1 activity page. Read aloud the first sentence: *What do we measure with a scale?* Read the possible answers. (Allow responses.) Then **say:** *Yes, we use a scale to measure weight, or how heavy something is.* Draw a circle around **weight**. Read aloud the second question. Make sure students know that the space between two places is distance. Guide students through the remaining questions.

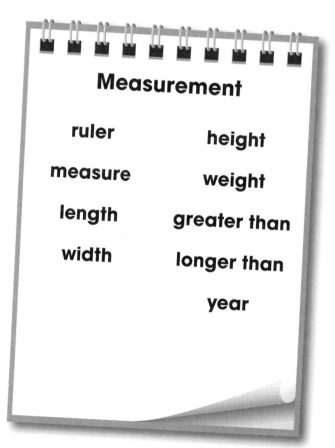

Measurement

ruler	height
measure	weight
length	greater than
width	longer than
	year

Name _____

Circle It!

Read the questions. Draw a circle around the answers.

What do we measure with a  ?   **weight**   **height**

scale

What is the space between two places?   **width**   **distance**

What does a  measure?   **height**   **time**

clock

Which is shorter?   **week**   **day**

Which is longer?   **minute**   **second**

Clock or Calendar

Cut out the words. Glue words that a clock measures under the clock. Glue words that a calendar measures under the calendar.

Clock	**Calendar**

---

day	hour	minute	month

second	week	year

Longer Than, Shorter Than

Cut out the rebuses and shuffle them. Deal the cards evenly between partners. Players turn over their top cards. The player whose picture shows something longer keeps both cards. Play until one player has won all of the cards. Then, play again with shorter pictures winning the hands.

| man | tree | dog | mouse |

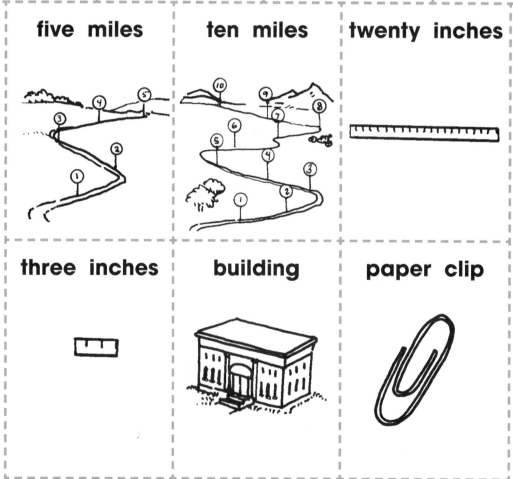

| five miles | ten miles | twenty inches |
| three inches | building | paper clip |

Greater Than or Less Than?

Draw a circle around the phrase that completes each sentence.

Twenty is   **greater than**   **less than**   ten.

Two miles is   **greater than**   **less than**   five miles.

Forty is   **greater than**   **less than**   sixty.

A month is   **greater than**   **less than**   a year.

Fifteen is   **greater than**   **less than**   seven.

Sixteen is   **greater than**   **less than**   fifteen.

Twelve pounds is   **greater than**   **less than**   thirty pounds.

A second is   **greater than**   **less than**   a minute.

Assessment

Draw a line to match the words with the tools that measure them.

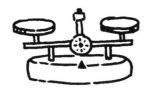

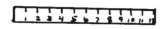

length

months

hours

weight

Draw something shorter than a tree.

Write a number that is greater than ten. _____